ONWARD

into

THE *LIGHT*

A True Story
of Profound Love, Devastating Loss,
and a Bond Unbroken by Death

To Monica,
Thank you so much for your
interest in our journey and for
hiring me for a job that I love!
With love + light,
Diane Santos

DIANE SANTOS

Cardinal Rules
——— PRESS ———

DEDICATION

For my Real Man...

Michael Tyrone "Tyger" Johnson

July 30, 1957 – July 30, 2014

~~ Loving You Always ~~

TABLE OF CONTENTS

ACKNOWLEDGMENTS

First and foremost, to my wonderful sons, Aaron and Mark, thank you for understanding as I navigate this journey of grief. You are my motivation to keep pushing toward the best version of myself and I'm proud to call each of you my son. Your caring hearts and quiet strength are a blessing from God.

Beloved family, without your love and support, I have no idea where I'd be. I am honored to be part of such a legacy of love, carried on by each generation. We were raised right! My love and thanks to you all and to my many wonderful friends.

My heartfelt gratitude to the Johnson family. Embracing my children and me as your own has helped us heal and we remain connected to Tyger through each of you. Thank you for helping make Tyger who he was and for sharing him with us.

Marley Gibson, best-selling author and freelance editor, thanks to your keen eye and amazing editing talents, my dream has become a reality. I have learned so much from you in such a short amount of time. A special thanks for never tiring of my questions – no matter how big or small.

Thank you, Lyn Ragan, author of *Wake Me Up! Love and the Afterlife,* for your guidance in the early stages of the self-publishing process. Your heartwarming story of love helped me find hope when it was desperately needed.

My sincere thanks to intuitive/medium, Laura Salafia, for validating what my soul already knew through your incredible gift. You restored peace to my heart and mind by relaying the messages of my Love. I will never be able to thank you enough for shifting my focus away from death and back to life.

To my friend, Lee, I thank you for bridging the gap between worlds. Your willingness to keep the lines of communication open is greatly appreciated. There are no coincidences, the three of us were brought together for an important purpose. My thanks for your continuing role in our journey.

Donna B., I don't think you realize the difference you've made in my life. By listening and witnessing so many "wow moments" with me, you encouraged me to keep believing. Your kindness and compassion come naturally from a place of genuine love. I am so grateful to have you as my friend.

As an unknowing messenger, Sophia Lynn, you keep Mike and me connected. Your beautiful, receptive soul hears his whispers and delivers them with pure innocence. Mike will always watch over and guide you. Nani loves you. The three of us share a bond that will go on forever.

Last, but certainly not least, to the man who took me to new heights of love and happiness, thank you, baby. You are my inspiration, Michael "Tyger" Johnson, and the source of my confidence to reach for the moon and beyond. Words cannot express my love for you or my gratitude for what we share. I will miss you until you take my hand and we walk into eternity. Our story will never be finished, my love. It is fluid, timeless and ongoing.

CHAPTER ONE
An Unforgettable Day

I OPENED MY EYES and looked at the clock. It read 7:00 a.m. It could have been just like every other day, but it wasn't because today was Tyger's birthday.

He'd been given the nickname "Tyger" as a little boy and it had stuck with him. There were people who'd known him their entire lives—including some family members—and never realized his name was actually Michael. It didn't matter to me who called him what. The only thing I ever called him was "Baby," anyway.

Excitedly, I reached for the phone that was laying on the nightstand. My routine was the same every morning: wake up, look at the clock, pick up the phone, and call my love. More often than not, there was a text waiting for me before I could even dial his number; a few words of he'd sent during the night to let me know he was thinking of me. Waking up to those messages of love always helped me start my day with a smile.

Today was all about him, though, and that was my focus as I scrolled through my contacts to select "My Man" and then placed the call.

"Happy Birthday!" I said when he answered with his familiar, "Helllllllo." His reply was, "Birthday? It's my birthday?"

I jokingly answered, "Yes, it is. You know, at your age, memory is the first thing to go."

We went on with our conversation, looking forward to the plans we had for later in the day.

In the weeks leading up to this day, I'd struggled with what to get him. What do you buy for the man who has everything? Whenever he wanted something, he just went out and got it so it wasn't as if he needed anything. I had pretty much made it my mission to change his opinion of birthdays and holidays, which he usually referred to as "just another day." Oh, he certainly knew how to make a big deal out of special days when it came to me, he just wasn't comfortable with anyone making a fuss over him.

I knew I wanted to make him a nice meal, so, in the meantime, I asked what he'd like for his birthday dinner. As a man who lived alone, he really enjoyed a home-cooked meal and I enjoyed making it for him. He loved my lasagna, so he decided that was what he wanted. Dinner was all set, but I still had no clue of what to do about a gift. That was until I found out the Drum Corps International (DCI) World Championships were being shown live at a local movie theater the week after his birthday. He was a huge fan of professional drum corps and had been a part of one in our hometown as a teenager. He owned several DCI performances on DVD and played them often. We had seen one together and I was so impressed with the intricacy of the moves and the discipline involved in the formations all while playing instruments. It was an amazing thing to witness.

This was something he really enjoyed and never in a million years would he see this gift coming. It was the perfect "Wow" gift.

I purchased the tickets online, printed the flyer describing the event, and put both items in the envelope with his card. I also bought him a new coffee mug because we were both coffee lovers and really enjoyed our first cup of the day. I ordered him a small cake and hoped I could contain my excitement until his birthday got here because I was sure he'd love it all.

We each went about our day after the morning call. He had things to do and I wanted to get the lasagna together so I could just put it in the oven later that afternoon. As the day went on, we exchanged our usual texts every time something popped into our minds that we wanted to share. Even if it was a quick "thinking 'bout u" or "love u lots," texting each other was something we did multiple times a day.

He had recently joined Facebook, so he was new to social media and enjoying all the birthday wishes he was getting. Navigating his way around his recently acquired laptop was new to him, as well, and he had moments of frustration with that. I'd get a call from time to time and he'd say, "Well, this thing's about five minutes from flying off my back porch." That was my cue to stop by and help him with whatever it was he was trying to do. After a few minutes of explaining things, he'd decide to hold off on tossing it just yet.

He couldn't believe how many people were posting birthday messages on his wall and he was having a great time replying to all of them. The funny thing about that was when he first had me set up his page, he didn't intend to post or comment on anything.

He said, "I heard about these Facebook creepers. They read what everyone's writing and find out everyone's business, but never comment on anything. I wanna be a creeper, too."

That sure didn't last long as he was commenting and posting left and right. As a matter of fact, he posted a few words in response to the many birthday wishes he was getting, written as only he could:

"Heyyy, thank you all! My b-day wish is that we all have a blessed day and may you all come thru and break me off $500-$600 a piece... you know... birthday type thing. Thanks!"

I read it and laughed. It was so "him."

I called him and said, "I hate to interrupt your busy social life. I'm just letting you know I'm taking Markie out to lunch. I'll meet you here at five-thirty for dinner."

My youngest son, Mark, was spending a few weeks during summer vacation at his dad's house across town. As a teenage boy, calling his mother every once in a while wasn't exactly high on his list of priorities, and it simply wasn't "cool" for a sixteen-year-old to hang out with his mom. He did enjoy going out to eat, though, so I figured a bribe of food was a good way to steal some time with him. Tyger was glad to hear Mark and I were having lunch.

"Okay, baby. Enjoy. I'll see you later," he responded.

When it was nearly 5:30 p.m., I decided to cut the lasagna. It had been out of the oven for a while and had rested long enough so it was safe to portion out. I'd learned the hard way about cutting lasagna before letting it cool—what a mess— and I wanted the squares to stand up on the plate like the picture on the pasta box.

"I made lasagna for Mike's birthday," I said to my son, Aaron, as he got ready for work. "I'll leave some in the fridge if you want any tonight or tomorrow."

I heard him say, "Okay, Mom. Thanks," as he went out the door. He was backing out of the parking lot across the street as Tyger pulled in and they waved to each other. A moment or so later I heard a voice in the living room.

"Hello? Anybody home?" as Tyger came in.

"I'm in here," I said from the kitchen, then greeted him with a great big birthday kiss. "Go ahead and have a seat." I was so anxious to see his reaction to his gift and wasn't waiting another minute.

He settled into his usual spot on the couch and I gave him his card and gift. I was right next to him as he opened them, my heart pounding with anticipation. He read the card first, every word of it, and then asked if I had written it myself because he said it was so perfect. The flyer with the info about the drum corps event was folded so he held it in his hand for a minute and asked, "What's this?"

It was obvious he was doing this on purpose to torture me. "Open it and find out," I said.

He unfolded it slowly and I could see his expression changing as he began to realize what it was. After a few seconds, he wore the biggest smile and I was thrilled.

"You're really gonna go with me to this?" he asked.

"Of course, I will, but if it was golf you were a fan of, I'd be sending you alone because golf is about as exciting as watching paint dry."

We laughed at my remark then we kissed and he hugged me tight. He always gave the best hugs. He was so happy and thankful for his gift. Everything was perfect.

The two of us sat at the table with soft jazz playing on the stereo, great conversation, enjoying dinner and being together. He told me he had taken a power nap before he arrived which wasn't something he normally did in the middle of the day. As he put it, "It's my birthday, so why not?"

He stayed for a while and then I asked if he wanted a small piece of his cake for dessert.

"No, I'm way too full from the meal. How 'bout you come by a little later with the rest of the lasagna and everything. Maybe eight-thirty or so?" He'd made it clear when he first asked for lasagna that he needed enough for "a few days." I was already anticipating the texts in the coming days to let me know every time he had another piece.

"Sounds good," I said. "I'll shoot you a message when I'm on my way."

He left and I went into the kitchen to do the dishes. I figured I'd be getting in late tonight and there was no way I'd be cleaning when I got home. If I didn't get them done now, they'd be sitting there waiting for me in the morning and I'd be kicking myself.

Just get them done now, Diane, you'll thank yourself in the morning.

I packed his things into a small box and left for his place just before 8:30 p.m. We lived close to each other, less than five minutes by car.

His door was unlocked when I got there. I walked through the living room, straight to the dining room, and put the box on the table along with my purse. I had that familiar excited feeling I got every time I arrived. He was in his room, right behind that door, anxiously waiting for me. Even after three years of being together, I still felt excitement every single time I was with him. His apartment was like my second home and I was so comfortable there.

As I walked into his room, he greeted me in his usual way, by saying in a kidding tone, "Hey, what are you doing here?"

I gave my usual response, "Well, I was in the neighborhood, so..."

The room was dark except for the light from the TV and the dim, flickering glow of the various battery-operated candles he had placed here and there. The air conditioner was on making the small room almost chilly. He was lying down, covered with a blanket.

He lifted it as he said, "C'mon, get in here."

I slid in next to him, feeling the warmth of his body and noticing the familiar scent of his clothes. I would always do the same thing: bury my face in the middle of his chest, take a deep breath, and say, "Mmm, your shirt smells so good."

He'd laugh, but I meant it. His shirts were always so fresh. It was a combination of his masculine scent and detergent that let me know I was home. Safe in his arms where I belonged. A place where nothing and no one could ever harm me in any way.

He wasn't a big fan of birthdays, never had been. To him, they were just another day. This one was different, though, and he decided he could learn to like them.

"So, you had a good day?" I asked.

"I had a great day!" was his answer.

In the background, *The Andy Griffith Show* was on, a favorite of ours to snuggle up in front of in the evenings on the TV Land channel. We loved the old programs and still laughed at them even though we'd seen the episodes over and over.

He told me again how surprised he was by his gift. I said I was impressed by his self-control, he hadn't asked even once where we were going since the day I told him to clear his schedule for Thursday, August 7th because we had plans.

"It might've seemed like I was in control," he said. "But, I had all kinds of crazy ideas about where you might be taking me." We laughed, which was something we did constantly. We had a wonderful ability to make each other laugh and that was one of many reasons I'd fallen so deeply in love with him.

We talked, watched TV, expressed our love, and simply enjoyed each other.

At one point, he said—his exact words–to me, "You have no idea how good it feels to go about my day knowing I've got a good girl."

That was so beautiful to hear and brought an instant smile to my face. By this time, the *King of Queens* was on, which meant it was 9:00 p.m.

Ten minutes into the show, he said, "I need to sit up."

"What's wrong?" I asked.

"I'm having trouble breathing. If I sit up, it might help."

Less than a year earlier, he'd been diagnosed with Congestive Heart Failure. He was taking his medications, monitoring his weight, and trying to eat healthier. This shortness of breath had happened a couple of times over the past few weeks, only while he was laying down. Usually, if he got up or went outside for some air, it would help and he'd get his breathing back under control. The next morning he'd wake up as though nothing had ever happened and feel like his normal self.

Still, I was worried.

Why was this happening?

I asked him to contact his cardiologist because this wasn't normal. Besides, it had happened the night before last. He'd gotten up and stood outside for some air and was able to get his breathing back to normal. The following morning, which was Tuesday, he finally took my advice and spoke with the cardiologist's office and had an appointment for Friday.

Today was only Wednesday and it was happening... again.

He stood out on the porch and I asked, "Should we go to the Emergency Room?"

He shouted, "No!" which startled me because he never raised his voice.

I stepped back into the living room, thinking I'd give him a moment or two. This had happened before and he was always fine after a few minutes. I had no reason to think this time would be any different. The last thing I wanted to do was make things worse. He already wasn't feeling well and didn't need me adding more stress to the situation.

He had moved further down on the porch, out of sight from the door. A few seconds later, I leaned out of the doorway to check on him. I was shocked when I saw he'd begun vomiting and was struggling to get air into his lungs.

He managed to get out, "Call 911!"

Without hesitation, I ran to the dining room for my phone—which took mere seconds—dialed the number, and as I reached the front door, I heard a loud thud. He had fallen straight back onto the porch.

I screamed into the phone, "Please help! Please send help!" I gave his address, completely frantic and terrified, begging the dispatcher to please do something for him. "I don't think he's breathing! Should I try turning him on his side? He's not breathing!"

She spoke firmly to me, explaining how to do chest compressions. "Put one hand on top of the other with the base of your hand in the middle of his chest. Now, press down and count 1,2... 1,2. Keep counting out loud with me."

I did as she told me, straddled Tyger's body and pressed down as hard as I could while holding the phone to my ear with my shoulder. "1,2... 1,2..." I counted as I heard the sirens getting closer. At one point, he made a move which gave me hope. "His mouth opened. Does that mean he's breathing?" I asked, hoping she'd say it was a good sign.

"Just keep going and keep counting out loud," she said.

"Oh, my God. His mouth is full. Won't he choke? Shouldn't he be on his side?"

Again, the dispatcher was firm. "Keep pressing as hard as you can. Don't move him and count with me. 1,2... 1,2..."

As I continued, the tears streamed down my face and I searched for any sign of life. He was staring straight up but not at me. His eyes looked so empty, but my mind was saying, "I know you're in there, baby. Just hold on. Help is coming."

I persisted with the compressions until the EMTs were standing next to me and took over. I hung up the phone and one of the paramedics took me aside to get information... his name, medical history, and details of what had happened. He was surrounded by several people all working on him as he laid there on the porch.

"Is he breathing?" I kept asking, but no one answered. Rightly so, they were focused on him.

Finally, a fireman walked over and spoke in a gentle tone, "He isn't doing well right now. We need to intubate him and this could be unpleasant. Why don't you step inside while we get him ready for transport?"

I did as he suggested. Although I'd heard everything he'd said to me, my mind chose to acknowledge one line in particular, "He's *not doing well*, which means he's still with us." That thought provided some relief so I chose to focus on that. Then, it occurred to me I should notify his family. I made two calls, one to his nephew and one to his best friend. I told them everything I knew and asked them to meet us at the hospital. I also called my best friend, my cousin, Angy.

Her husband answered and I spoke with my voice shaking. "Dewayne, something's wrong with Tyger. The ambulance is here and they're working on him but he doesn't look good."

He asked where Tyger lived and I managed to explain. "Angy is getting ready for work, but I'll tell her what happened and we'll be right over."

A few minutes later, I saw Dewayne pull up. "You wanna ride with me to the hospital?" he yelled from across the street.

"No, I'll drive my car. I'll meet you there."

They had Tyger in the ambulance, so I got into my car, planning to follow right behind. He lived on a narrow, dead-end road. I was parked at the end and blocked in by the fire truck. There was no way of turning the big rig around, so they had to back all the way out. Waiting for that fire truck to get out of my way felt like an eternity.

Sitting in my car, slowly making my way to the main road, I was so angry with myself. "Damn it! Why didn't I ride with Dewayne? What was I thinking? This is taking too long."

Finally, I was able to head to the hospital. My mind raced as I drove. Was this really happening? Images of him lying on the porch kept flashing through my mind. My big, strong man, just lying there helplessly. Had I done enough? I replayed the events leading up to the ambulance arriving and remembered doing exactly as the dispatcher told me. Why hadn't he awakened even after the EMTs worked on him? Why didn't I stand right there as they put him in the ambulance? Why, why, why? There were no answers, so I began to pray. I never stopped praying out loud the whole ride there, begging God to *please* let him be all right. I asked my parents in Heaven to help me, to save him, to do any and everything they could. Screaming to my love, "Please baby, please fight! Please hold on!"

When I pulled into the hospital parking lot, I saw Angy and Dewayne standing outside. Angy walked in with me and we approached the woman at the desk to ask about Tyger's condition. She said she had no information, but a nurse would be out to speak to us. In the meantime, I stepped over to another desk and asked if they needed Tyger's insurance. Back at the house, while they worked on him on the porch, I had gone into his room to grab his wallet and all his medications. I figured they'd need all of this and would want to know what medications he was taking. I gave the woman at the desk the insurance card and a nurse came out and asked if we'd like to sit in the family waiting room.

Angy and I were the only ones there at the time, we followed the nurse into a very small room. She asked if she could get us anything and we said no. She left us there and shut the door behind her.

Something felt wrong and I said to Angy, "I don't have a good feeling about this. Why did they put us in this tiny room?"

She said, "Don't worry, I'm sure he'll be fine. They just wanted to give us some privacy."

We sat and prayed together and I felt numb, unable to even cry. Up until that point, I'd been reacting instinctively to everything happening, however, the shock had begun to set in.

Tyger's nephew and niece arrived along with three of his close friends. I began telling them everything that had happened. We were all speculating on what could be going on and how he was doing.

After what seemed like forever, the door finally opened. Angy and I were sitting on a couch while Tyger's niece and a family friend were across from us and the men were standing. All conversation stopped as the doctor walked in, followed by a nurse. I searched for any sign of hope, desperately trying to read their expressions.

The doctor asked, "Is everyone here a relative of Michael's?"

Tyger's nephew answered, "No. Can you speak with the family in private?"

"Yes. Would the family members please step into the main waiting area?"

We followed the doctor into a corner of the large, empty room. Both of my legs felt weak and my stomach churned with each step. There was silence as he began to explain.

"Michael was in serious condition when the emergency personnel arrived. They worked on him during transport and continued trying everything possible here. Unfortunately, we were not able to get him back. I'm sorry to tell you, Michael didn't make it."

My chest tightened as I processed his words. Struggling to draw breath, it felt as though time had stopped. My heart began to race and the sound of blood pounding in my ears with each beat thrust me back into the moment.

"Michael didn't make it."

Four words that shattered my world into a million pieces.

I remember shouting, "*Nooooooo!*" before collapsing into Angy's arms, flooded with tears and disbelief.

Four words.

Four little words and, just like that, life as I knew it was over.

Four words that took away everything that was familiar.

Four words which set me on a path to the unknown.

The one and only thing I did know, was *nothing* would ever be the same again.

CHAPTER TWO
Friendship and Beyond

"IF I EVER HAD A WOMAN LIKE YOU, I'd be doing ninety every day to get home to her."

I can't even tell you how many times I heard those words. I'd always laugh, though, chalking it up to a flirtatious line. Tyger and I both worked in food service at a large casino for many years and would see each other in passing. A quick hello was usually the extent of our conversations, but every now and then, I'd stop at his station and talk for a few minutes. We'd grown up in the same town and our families knew each other. Since there was a ten-year age difference, we hadn't traveled in the same circles growing up.

One day, he mentioned the names of my older cousins, telling me he knew them, but wondered where they'd been hiding me. I laughed and said I was probably still playing with Barbie dolls when he started noticing girls.

It didn't take long for me to begin realizing how easy he was to talk to. For people who didn't know him, his appearance was quite intimidating. At six-foot-five and 420 pounds, his size could be cause for caution. Yet, when he spoke, there was something that let you know right away this was a good guy. I think what first impressed me was his ability to listen. I felt like he listened to what I was saying with genuine interest and he never jumped in with a comment or interrupted. When I finished what I was saying, he'd respond with something that made perfect sense. Whether it was advice or his take on what was being said, his responses always had substance.

In the outside world, he was Tyger, but at work, he was Mike or Big Mike. His charismatic personality drew people in and it was a rare occurrence to find him at his workstation alone. It was nearly impossible for anyone to walk by without stopping for a few words. These weren't just people of a particular group or type either. Old, young, male, female, black, white, brown, or whatever else you could think of, they were all there. I often told him he had the most eclectic bunch of acquaintances I'd ever seen. Each and every one of them was completely comfortable with him. He spoke a universal language called *the plain truth* without any bull and it resonated with anyone he had contact with. Not to say there weren't a few who were put off by his direct way of speaking, but they were definitely in the minority.

As much as people were drawn to him, he had spent the majority of his life as somewhat of a loner. He would be the first to tell you many may have heard his name, but few actually knew him. Something he laughingly referred to as, "The myth of Tyger Johnson." He told me he preferred to live his life privately and wasn't a big fan of people in general. My response was regardless how he felt about them, everyone certainly seemed to love him.

Tyger had a wealth of life experience to draw on. He made no excuses or apologies for his past. He'd made mistakes and he owned up to them, learned from them. The fact that he'd experienced so much gave him the ability to speak with conviction. You knew when he spoke about something it wasn't because he'd read it in a book or learned it in a classroom. He had actually *lived* it. I respected that raw honesty and admired his willingness to speak freely about any bad decisions he'd made and the effect they'd had on his life.

There was an expression he used often: "If the truth hurts, say ouch."

What that meant was he would always give it to you straight and he didn't believe in sugar-coating anything. I admired this quality because I had always been one to tip-toe around other people's feelings. He didn't do any tip-toeing, yet what he said was generally received quite well. Even if their feelings were slightly bruised, most people usually realized he was on point.

The interactions between us soon became longer and more frequent. I'd found myself being drawn to him and wanting to hear his take on whatever it was I was thinking. I enjoyed our conversations and hearing about his life. Some of his experiences were so far from anything I'd ever been through, yet he had a way of telling a story that put you right there. You could picture exactly what was going on at the time and you couldn't wait to hear what came next.

As much as I enjoyed listening, what I really loved was the way he always made me laugh. So much of what he said was funny or just plain unexpected and you couldn't help but crack up. That continued throughout our entire relationship. It wasn't superficial laughter, either. Most of the time, it was eye-watering, belly-hurting, air-gasping laughter. He enjoyed my sense of humor, as well, and we'd go back and forth saying the funniest things.

At this stage, I was having a great time, sharing stories with this wonderful friend who was brutally honest and never failed to entertain me. Everything was completely innocent on my part, but he would later admit his intentions went way beyond friendship. Not that he tried all that hard to hide them. He never hesitated to tell me how attractive he found me or the way he felt I should be treated.

One day, the large dishwasher was malfunctioning and there were suds everywhere coming out the sides of the machine all over the floor. When I got back to his work area, I said, "Wow, I could take a bubble bath in the dish room."

He stopped what he was doing and closed his eyes.

"What are you doing?"

He said, "Shhh... don't ruin my vision. I'm picturing you in the bubbles wearing nothing but my football jersey."

Instantly, I felt my cheeks began to heat up from blushing so badly. I said to him, "Guess I left myself wide open for that one."

Sometimes I could be a bit naive.

Growing up in the same town helped us feel connected. We knew many of the same people, if not personally, then we knew the family. This familiarity meant we didn't have to explain the details of every situation since we'd had some similar experiences. We also spoke often about the different paths our lives had taken. As I said, he didn't cover up the rough patches in his life; whether it was past relationships or actions that had landed him in prison. Then, there was me... the quiet girl who always did well in school and had never been arrested in her life. He often said if we ever did get together it would leave many people scratching their heads, wondering how it came about. He referred to us as "The Beauty and the Beast," not based on how we looked, but on our varied experiences.

At first glance, we couldn't have seemed more unalike, yet that was far from the actual truth. I never judged him and I had so much respect for his honesty and his ownership of his past. I also shared with him my shortcomings, despite my "good girl" reputation. I'd made plenty of mistakes and done things I wasn't proud of. We communicated so easily right from the beginning as if we'd known each other forever.

One day, while I was walking in the park, he called and asked if we could meet there to talk. I was hesitant because we'd never been together outside of work. I nervously said yes and he was on his way. This would later become a funny story when he shared the details of his ride there.

"Remember that day you said we could meet at the park? Well, I ran two red lights and a stop sign getting to you after you said yes." He was laughing, but I actually believed he was telling the truth.

Anyway, he came and picked me up and we took a long ride. It was then he told me he'd like us to be more than friends.

He made it clear he wasn't looking for anything serious, but would like to spend time together outside of work and see where it led us. Since I enjoyed his company already, I was interested in finding out where it would go.

I'll never forget the first time I went to his place. I could not believe he had decorated it himself. In fact, I said to him, "You had a woman help you do all this."

"No, I did not," he said. "This is all me."

I kept telling him how nice it was and how good he was at decorating

He said, "So, you're saying I'm gay?"

"No," I responded. "I'm just saying I love your style."

Our tastes were so similar, yet not exactly the same. His attention to detail exceeded my own and I was amazed by the ideas he'd come up with. I remember thinking, "I would've done something like that, but how did he think to do it that way?"

We talked about how we both liked balance and whatever decorating we did had to "feel right." He shared with me that every time he changed something in a room, he'd have to step out and then return to see how it felt. I couldn't believe he said that because I had always done the same thing. Here I was thinking I was the only one who did the quick "out and in test," but he did it, too.

He was full of surprises. Such a great example of how much you can miss if you judge a book by its cover. Who would've every expected this massive guy to have such a natural talent for decorating? There were so many dimensions to this man and I had barely scratched the surface.

As our feelings for one another began to grow stronger, we became intimate. The details of those private moments belong to us alone. What I will say is we connected so well on every level; physically was no exception. I can best describe it as the most attentive, passionate tenderness I'd ever known. A transcendent experience for each of us; a "knowing" without having to verbally express what the other needed. Our feelings were intensified through our mutual enjoyment. Neither of us held anything back because we felt no judgment. It was simply pure happiness and a true connection at the deepest level.

I mentioned to him once how talented he was in that area and asked, "Did you go to school to learn this stuff?"

He said, "No, but in case you ever decide you've had enough of me, I wanna make sure I get it all in."

We laughed and I said, "Had enough of you? Shoot, good luck getting rid of me. I'm not going anywhere."

Little did we know then how thankful we'd be for his way of thinking and for applying this logic like he did. We approached everything with the intention of "getting it all in."

I told him once what a good listener he'd been back when we were just friends and how it played a major role in his gaining my trust.

He said, "You thought I was listening? A few words into whatever you were saying and you sounded like Charlie Brown's teacher. *Wah wah, wah wah* was all I heard. I was looking at your beautiful face thinking what I'd do to you if I ever got the chance."

Well, he'd done a great job of hiding it because all his responses made perfect sense. He asked if I'd ever noticed he would always stop working and put his knife down whenever I came by to talk. He said he did it because he was so distracted by what he was seeing and thinking, he worried he'd lose a finger while slicing the meat. Apparently, he didn't dare pick the knife up until after I'd walked away.

We kept the status of our relationship to ourselves. I was sure people had their suspicions, especially at work where we spent so much time talking, but we left it open to speculation, not confirming or denying what was happening between us. He told me how some of the guys were offering him advice about how to approach me. They all knew how interested he was, but had no idea we were already involved.

He was told, "Go ahead and ask her out to dinner or a movie. She's feeling you. She'll say yes. Just start off slowly."

He said to me, "They think I'm scared and I should stop the bullshit and just ask you out." By this point, we were way past the dinner and a movie stage. Still, it showed us something wonderful was happening between us and it was noticeable to those we knew. His thoughts were that people would be happy for us once the news got out because we were well-liked so they'd be glad to see us together. I would come to realize later that he was exactly right.

We'd each had two failed marriages, as well as other past relationships, so we came together carrying our own baggage. Initially, this may have been cause for caution, but we'd been truthful about everything. We shared our experiences and how they'd affected our lives. It was our openness that allowed us to leave our baggage in the past where it belonged. Neither of us felt the need to punish the other for past hurts we'd experienced. Our honesty and openness allowed us to see one another as we truly were rather than some reincarnation of a past relationship gone wrong.

For the first time in my life, I was actually dating. I had this wonderful man who showered me with loads of attention, affection, and, most of all, his time. This was completely new to me; a man who shared his time willingly rather than feeling like he had to in order to avoid an argument. He went places with me because he *wanted* to. We loved to go out to eat; breakfast dates, lunch, dinner, it didn't matter. We went shopping together to places like the Christmas Tree Shop and HomeGoods.

A favorite memory of mine is from a breakfast date at Denny's. The weather was nice so I wore a mini skirt. On our way out, we passed a table full of construction workers. We got outside and he says, "I feel sorry for them. They wanted to turn around and look at you so badly after you walked by, but they didn't dare with my big ass walking right behind you. Go back in and act like you forgot something so they can have their look."

I told him he was nuts. There was no way I was going back to having a bunch of guys stare at my behind. It was a funny moment, but one of many ways he showed me how proud he was of his lady.

One night, as I was getting dressed to head over to his place, he called and said, "Be ready in five minutes, I'm coming to get you." Trust me, when he said *five minutes*, he meant it, so I knew to be prepared. After he picked me up, he got on the highway. A couple of towns away, he pulled into a hotel and went in to pay for a room.

"What's the occasion?" I asked.

"No occasion. I just thought we'd do something different."

He grabbed a small bag from the back seat and we went in to get settled.

The first thing he did when we walked in was to snatch the comforter off the bed with one hand and fling it onto the floor across the room.

"What was that for?" I asked.

He said to me, "I saw on the news these hotels never wash those things. They only change the sheets. Better safe than sorry."

I laughed at the way he'd tossed it like it was a small handkerchief. He pulled out the bag he'd brought and inside were snacks and drinks for us. I was so touched and wondered if I was dreaming. Was this actually happening? I mean, really, how many guys are thoughtful enough to be so spontaneous and even think to bring snacks, too? What an incredible night; one I'll never, ever forget.

Since we both worked during the day, we most often would get together in the evenings after dinner time. That was "lay down time" as he called it where we'd snuggle in his bed in front of the TV, talking, and, of course, there was plenty of laughter. His bedroom was two rooms separated by curtains he'd hung across the large, open doorway. The extra room was used for storage, so we seldom went in there.

One night, we went to lay down and I noticed his pillows were gone from the bed. When I asked him where they were, he said, "They've moved on to a better place."

I didn't bother asking any further. I figured he was getting new ones or something. After a few minutes, he asked me to go into the spare room to grab a blanket. When I stepped through the curtains, I couldn't believe my eyes. He had bought a brand new bedroom set.

I asked, "When did you have time to do this?"

He chuckled. "I've been working on it for a few days."

When I turned the light on to check things out, there sat the pillows on the new bed. They were definitely in a better place, just like he'd said.

That room became our oasis, nicely decorated with a fashionable comforter set and matching curtains. His style was second to none and, once again, my mind was blown. He was so excited telling me about shopping for his bedding.

He asked, "Do you know what a sham is?"

I answered, "Yes, they cover your pillows kind of like a fancy pillow case."

He said, "Well, I didn't know what they were. There was a lady in the same aisle so I asked her what they were and she explained. I've got shams now."

That became a running joke with us.

Tyger was one of the most thoughtful, giving people I'd ever met. His biggest concern was always my comfort and happiness. He used to say, "I'm living well, so my girl should be, too."

I'd be leaving his house and he'd say, "Grab that money I left on the table. It's a few dollars for you to get an iced coffee or something."

I'd put it in my purse and get home to find it was fifty dollars or more. I'd call and ask him how much he thought they charged for iced coffee. He would laugh and say he wanted me to have a few dollars in my pocket.

Many times, he would call and tell me to meet him at the gas station. I'd pull up to the pump and he'd drive in behind me. We'd talk while he filled my tank, then a quick kiss, and he'd send me on my way. More than once, he had my son, Aaron, meet him at the gas station and filled his tank, as well. One day I arrived at work and realized I'd forgotten to leave my granddaughter's car seat at home for Aaron. This was a problem because I knew he'd need it later. Tyger's shift was ending, so I asked him to grab it and drop it off at my house. A few days later, we were meeting for breakfast. When I arrived at the restaurant, he got out of his car holding a brand new car seat.

He said, "I needed you to have your own. Tell Aaron to keep the other one."

This wasn't any old car seat, either. It was a deluxe model with two cup holders. I asked him what she would need with those and I soon found out. She was forever using them, whether it was a drink, toys, etc. He loved hearing about the times she would tell me, "Put that in my cup holder," referring to a toy or anything else she was bringing along for the ride.

My youngest son, Mark, turned sixteen and was anxious to start driving. I'd taken him out a few times in my car, but only at the cemetery because I was too nervous to let him drive on the road.

One day Tyger said, "Tell Mark I'll come by and get him on Sunday to take him out driving."

He picked him up in his SUV and took him to a back road with hills, lots of curves, and not much traffic. Mark told me he told him to "get behind the wheel and show him what he could do." This became a regular thing for several weeks. He'd pick Mark up on Sunday afternoon and they'd go out for a lesson. Tyger told me Mark did well without "his mother stressing him out."

Months later, at my family reunion, Tyger let Mark drive his vehicle on the road surrounding the area of the park where we were. As he was parking, Tyger told him to pull in a different spot. Mark gave it a little too much gas and ended up hitting the back of another vehicle parked in front of him. All we heard was *crunch* and my heart sank.

There was no damage to the other car, but the front of Tyger's had a small dent and the plastic around one of the headlights was broken. I waited for him to get upset, but he was calm as could be. My poor son looked so nervous and was ready to get out, but Tyger asked, "Where are you going? Don't worry about that. Just park it. You know what to do."

The car he'd hit belonged to a cousin I hadn't met before and she laughed about it, telling us about the fender benders she had while learning to drive. Tyger walked over and picked up the pieces of plastic that had fallen off his car and said, "A little Super Glue on these and it'll be good as new."

That was the end of it. He never got angry or said another word about it.

As good as he was to my boys, it was my granddaughter, Sophia (Aaron's daughter), who absolutely stole his heart. My boys didn't know him as Tyger—they called him Mike—and to

Sophia, he was "Mikey." It is often said children are excellent judges of character. They can spot a phony from a mile away and recognize goodness as quickly. Adults could sometimes be intimidated by Tyger's size, but not this little girl. She knew he was good and they formed an incredible bond. He always kept her engaged, talking to her, asking questions, listening to what she had to say. He loved to make up stories to tell her then I'd laugh when she'd ask detailed questions and he'd have to think fast for answers. She was so comfortable around him and loved when we went to visit him. He had an electric keyboard, which she called a piano, and she loved to play it.

One day, we were home and I told her he was coming over. I was on the phone with him so she says nonchalantly, "Tell him to bring the piano." When he arrived, guess what was in the back seat? He brought her outside with him and in they walked with the keyboard.

A few minutes later she says, "Hey, Mikey, why you got chips in your car?"

Back out he went and gave her the potato chips he'd bought for himself. He looked at me and said, "I think she's got me wrapped around her little finger."

She loved to invite him for Sunday breakfast. The few times he wasn't able to make it she was so worried about what he'd have to eat. I believe she thought if he didn't eat with us, he didn't eat at all. He always called her his "favorite little person" and she was welcome to go anywhere with us anytime. We'd go to a restaurant and the waitress would bring a child's placemat and crayons to the table. The two of them would sit there coloring together and drawing pictures while we waited for our food. Then, when our meals arrived, they would trade things, bacon for sausage, or French fries for a piece of chicken. There were always negotiations going on with those two.

He showed up at our door one day with a pink tricycle for her. When she outgrew it, he replaced it with a pink "Hello Kitty" bicycle. They simply enjoyed being together and she always knew she was included. On Valentine's Day, when he brought me flowers, he also had a small plant for her so she wouldn't feel left out. It was funny because my flowers died after a few days, as cut flowers do, but her plant grew and grew and is still healthy today.

Right before his birthday in 2013, Sophia said to him, "Mike, what do you want on your cake, a dinosaur or flowers?"

He thought for a moment and said, "Well, with those choices, I guess I'll take a dinosaur."

So, she says, "Okay, we'll get you a dinosaur cake."

Of course, I had already ordered his cake days earlier and was having a picture of him and I put onto it. We had to get a dinosaur on there so Soph and I went to the store and she decided on this plastic T-Rex. We picked up his cake, stuck the dinosaur on top, and then headed over to his place with his gifts and some balloons. As he was about to blow out the candles, she reminded him to make a wish.

He pretended he couldn't think of one, so he said, "Soph, you make a wish for me."

She squeezed her eyes shut and said, "I wish I was a beautiful princess."

He and I laughed so hard, we assumed she'd make a wish on his behalf, not completely leave him out. It was so precious and I told him if he woke up the next morning in a princess dress, it was his own fault for letting her make his wish.

Off she went exploring every room of his apartment. In his bedroom, he had this sculpture of a tiny table with dogs seated around it playing a game of cards. She got the biggest kick out of how silly it was because everyone knows dogs can't play cards. Her favorite dog was a white poodle wearing a beret. She never put it down the whole time we were there.

Maybe a week or so later, the three of us went out to dinner. We were waiting for our food when he pulled the T-Rex out of his pocket and proceeded to tell her this story.

"Soph, I have a problem and I need your help. Every day when I get home from work, I find the dinosaur crying. He keeps asking the dogs to let him play cards with them, but they won't let him. The white dog with the hat is really mean and calls him names. I don't know what to do because I have to go to work and he's so sad when I get home. Do you think he could stay with you so he doesn't have to be with those mean dogs?"

Well, let me tell you, she was completely enthralled with this story. First of all, how could those dogs she loved be so mean? Especially her favorite white poodle with the hat. The best part of this story wasn't her reaction; it was the family sitting at the table across from us. They had seen him take the dinosaur out of his pocket and overheard his story. The woman explained to me, at first, they were listening to see how long he could hold Sophia's attention, but after a few minutes, they were hanging on his every word, waiting to hear what happened next. That was him all right, Mr. Charisma. Of course, Sophia agreed to let the dinosaur stay with her. She never quite looked at those figurine doggies the same way again. The way he spoke to my granddaughter always made her feel important like she mattered. She was never dismissed or ignored in any way and she held their bond tight in her heart.

Since he walked into my life, each day was better than the one before. Just when I thought I couldn't possibly be happier, he found new ways to make me smile. He told me up until he met me, he'd always lived his life by design. Everything was set up to be as stress and drama-free as possible. If something disrupted his way of living, he simply removed it.

He said, "I'm doing well, my place looks great, vehicles are nice, but one piece is missing. I needed a cherry on top."

That was what I became in his world—his cherry on top—and he called me that often.

The smile never left my face and I was head over heels in love with a man who had me floating on a cloud. Although I knew I was walking around, I swear, it felt as if my feet never actually touched the ground. Giving and receiving love completely and in every way imaginable was a brand new experience for both of us.

In one another, we had found our soulmate.

CHAPTER THREE
Shattered Dreams

"MICHAEL DIDN'T MAKE IT."

What was this doctor saying?

What did those words even mean?

"Less than two hours ago, we were laying in each other's arms, now you're telling me 'Michael didn't make it.' This is impossible, it has to be a horrible nightmare. Today is his birthday, someone go in there and *wake him up!*"

That was what my brain was saying shortly after hearing the doctor's words. The tears were falling, but my mind could not comprehend what was happening. I mean, he hadn't even had any birthday cake yet or used his new coffee mug.

This can't be true. We have plans next week to go the theater and see the drum corps championships. We have things to do so there is no way "Michael didn't make it."

Even as I was having these thoughts, externally I was behaving as though I believed what the doctor told us. I was crying and experiencing pain, but I was so conflicted because it couldn't possibly be true.

The doctor was very compassionate. He took me aside and assured me Michael hadn't suffered. In my mind, though, he *had* suffered, at least for a few seconds before we lost him. The doctor explained I had done what I could with the compressions and the EMTs had worked very hard to get him back the whole ride to the hospital.

The official cause of death was listed as heart failure. I heard the words as he spoke, yet at the time, they didn't have much meaning.

The doctor asked if any of us would like to go in and see him and Tyger's niece and I said yes. I walked through the Emergency Department feeling as if it was totally surreal. A nurse led us into a room. He was lying there so peacefully with a sheet covering his legs. His arms were relaxed and resting at his sides and his eyes were closed like he was in a deep sleep.

I leaned in and kissed him, but it was so different... no reaction, no response at all. His body was there: the arms that once held me, the hands that had caressed me, the lips which kissed mine... and yet, something was missing.

In that instant, I felt broken and completely alone.

His family began arriving at the hospital. As I hugged them, I kept repeating how sorry I was. It didn't seem unusual for me to say that; those words were used as an expression of sympathy. The difference was, I didn't mean it that way. I was apologizing for not being able to save him. I had listened to the 911 dispatcher and did everything she'd said. I tried as hard as I could, but it still wasn't enough and I was so sorry.

In my state of mind, I fully expected his family to hate me and blame me for not saving him. Why wouldn't they? I was already blaming myself. I would find out later they didn't feel that way at all even though in those moments and in my fragile state, it seemed as if I had failed him and it was all my fault.

Eventually, I made my way back home. I sat slumped on the couch in my dimly-lit living room. Time didn't matter, so I have no idea how long I sat there. I tried to understand what had happened. I knew it was true because I had seen him, touched him, kissed him and recognized what was missing. His physical body was there, but *he* was not. The part that made him who he was had left and all that remained was this shell which had housed the *real* him. All I kept thinking was "he was just sitting here, right here in this spot reading his card."

I went back and forth between uncontrollable crying and the silent numbness of shock. The house was completely quiet except for the ticking of the clock on the wall. I'd never noticed before how loud the clock was.

I was startled by the door opening. It was Aaron coming home from work. He took one look at me and asked, "Mom, what's wrong?"

Through my tears, I managed to say, "Mike died. He's gone."

Aaron's eyes opened wide as he took a step back from me and said, "No! No, he isn't. I saw him in the parking lot when I was leaving for work and he waved to me. He's not dead."

This wasn't making sense to him either. How could this have happened in the course of his shift at work? After a few seconds, the news seemed to sink in. I hugged my son and cried.

At some point, I got up from the couch, walked slowly into my bedroom, and laid on the bed. I didn't bother getting undressed or turning the light off. I simply laid there staring at the picture of Tyger and me hanging on the wall. This was always the last thing I saw at night and the first image that greeted me in the morning. I was sitting on his lap with both of us smiling and so happy. Seeing it now was so different and brought out varied emotions. I began to feel an unfamiliar ache in my chest. It was a sharp and stabbing along with a feeling in my stomach that I can only describe as excruciating nausea. Real, actual, physical discomfort combined with the deepest, most heartbreaking loneliness I've ever experienced.

It was around 5:00 a.m. when I finally dozed off and slept for about an hour. When I opened my eyes, I was still facing our picture and the overwhelming reality of losing him hit me with a crushing weight. The horror, the fear, and the unimaginable sadness in my soul to wake up in a world I did not recognize in any way. Everything I thought I knew was gone. Every heartbeat was a painful reminder that his was no longer beating. How could this possibly be true? Couldn't I call him and he'd answer? Hadn't he sent a text while I slept to tell me he loved me? How was I going to draw my next breath without him?

I reached for my phone the same way I'd done every morning for as far back as I could remember. This time was very different, though. Rather than calling him, I called my family to let them know Tyger had passed away.

The reaction was the same each time: total disbelief at what I was saying. Almost everyone knew it was his birthday the day before, so how could it be possible I was speaking such unbelievable words? Of course, I had to repeat what I was saying several times because it was so difficult to understand me through the tears. A couple of friends had shared the news of his passing on Facebook, so I was receiving messages from countless people. I would read the posts, but was completely unable to respond. Finally, I managed to post a message to everyone acknowledging their kindness and concern:

"Please know I see all the messages and posts and I truly appreciate all of you. A huge piece of my heart is gone and I'm lost right now. If I don't reply, please know how thankful I am for your prayers. I will love my Tyger until the end of time and even longer."

As the news spread, family members began calling and coming by to see me. Although I'm an only child that has never been an issue because I was blessed to be born into a large, close-knit family. They all rallied around me; aunts, uncles, cousins, you name it. Someone was always calling, visiting, leaving messages, sending cards. I was so thankful for the love they showed, whether it was stopping by with food or simply making sure I had everything I needed. If one of them called and I didn't answer, they had a whole network set up for contacting each other to see if anyone had spoken with me or driven by to see if I was home. They did everything they possibly could to make sure I knew they were there for me and I was loved. I received calls from friends I'd worked with at the casino and offers of help from so many. My support system was nothing short of amazing.

In addition to my own family, I received support from Tyger's family, as well. Even though they had experienced such an unexpected, devastating loss, they took the time to check on me. He was one of nine children; an older sister and his mother had passed away many years earlier, but he still had seven siblings along with his Dad.

One afternoon, several of his brothers and his brother-in-law came by. They wanted to see how I was doing and let me know how much I'd meant to their brother. I also spoke to his sisters, nieces, and nephews and they shared with me how they had never seen him as happy as he'd been since I'd come into his life. I was included in the decisions about his final arrangements and was invited to continue being a part of family functions. They considered me a member of the family and I was listed in his obituary as his "Soulmate and love of his life." Sophia was listed as his grandchild. What a blessing it was to know they didn't blame me in any way. In fact, they were happy I'd been there so he wasn't alone when it happened.

The funeral service was beautiful. It was held at Tyger's nephew's church. He's a pastor and delivered an amazing eulogy about the legacy his uncle had left behind. My sons and family members sat right by my side during this amazing outpouring of love. So many heartfelt words were said about the man who'd made my world a better place simply by being in it. Those who spoke took the time to describe the ways Tyger had touched their lives and what an amazing person and friend he was. I was unable to speak at the service. I knew it would be impossible for anyone to understand what I was saying through the tears. More than one family member thanked me for making him so happy. I'd written him a poem two years earlier for Christmas, so I printed out a copy and wrote a message to him. My boys added a few words and signed it, as did Sophia. I folded it and put it in Tyger's inside jacket pocket to be with him forever.

The cemetery was the most difficult part. I fell to my knees and laid across the casket. Half-crying, half-screaming, pouring out my heart. There was so much I needed to tell him and it didn't matter who was listening or who was there.

"Thank you for teaching me how to live and for bringing me up when I didn't even know I was down. Thank you for that, baby. You said you wanted to get it all in and we did, baby. We got it all in. I just wasn't ready for you to go. Sophia wants you to come back and I don't know what to tell that little girl."

I thanked God for blessing my life with this man and swore to live the rest of my days in a way that would honor him and his memory. After a while, I felt myself being lifted by my arms and as I got back on my feet I apologized to Tyger, "I'm sorry, baby. I know you didn't like anyone causing a scene. I'm sorry I did. I'll do better."

I was led away and was just about to my car before I realized it was two of my cousins who had lifted me off the ground and were helping me walk. Of all things to be going through my mind at that moment, I distinctly remember being very upset about Tyger being put in the ground because he didn't like bugs. That really bothered me.

Following the service, we went to a hall for the repast. There was so much food and so many people there, yet I remember feeling so completely alone. I could see everyone and hear their voices, but none of that mattered because Tyger was missing. I was so overwhelmed with sadness and longed for him to come through the door and explain that this had been a big misunderstanding and he was back.

I sat at a table slowly looking around the room trying to figure out what I was supposed to do next. People were speaking to me and even though I was answering, I was completely disconnected at the same time. Sitting there feeling numb with sadness. Empty and alone after the finality of leaving his body at the cemetery.

Up until that point, we'd been busy with arrangements and getting things in order. Everything was different now; there were no more discussions or plans to be made. He was buried and that was it.

Someone made me a plate and set it down in front of me. I pushed the food around with my fork and forced myself to take a few bites because I knew someone would be by to see if I'd eaten anything. I stayed a while and then went home and collapsed in tears again. Tyger's family had a large poster board made with his picture on it which was displayed at the funeral and the hall afterward. Friends and family signed their names and wrote messages to him. It was given to me to keep. When I got home, I read the words that were written to him and was reminded of how much he was loved. He'd made such an impact on so many people. Later in the afternoon, I drove back to the cemetery and sat in disbelief that he was there. The reality of it stared me right in the face, no denying it.

The days and weeks that followed were like a long, continuous nightmare. The silence was deafening without the sound of his voice. There was an ache I felt deep within that never went away. I fell asleep with it and woke up in the same agony. I lost ten pounds in less than two weeks because I could not eat. I literally had no appetite or desire for food whatsoever.

Family members were constantly bringing meals over, but it felt as though the muscles used for chewing didn't have the strength to work. I never once felt hungry either. The pain and longing overpowered everything else.

Another thing I was unable to do was to drink coffee. We'd always had that in common and spoke so often about enjoying "a nice cup of coffee." Tyger had given me so many mugs over the years and the most recent one was a birthday gift with the words "Queen of the Universe" printed on it. He said that's what I was to him and when he'd seen it on the shelf he had to get it for me. It took everything in me to look at that thing, let alone drink out of it.

I was consumed by how much I missed him and I couldn't stand existing without him. Nothing seemed to matter and all I wanted was "us" back. The empty space without him could not be filled by anything; words, visits, well wishes... nothing. Mornings seemed pointless and nights went on forever.

I still got up every day and dressed, but to do what? To go where? I was devastated and completely heartbroken. I would wake up feeling crushed like I couldn't take another step or breathe without him here. I would cry, pray, scream, pound my fists, but still felt lost, overwhelmed with pain and longing.

The love and concern from friends and family were appreciated. However, even though I was surrounded by many people, I felt completely alone. There were numerous offers of help, but the only one who could was my love and he wasn't here anymore. He was the person who always fixed things and made everything better. Without him here, every moment of my life felt unfamiliar. The sun wasn't as bright, colors seemed dull, music sounded flat, and absolutely nothing made sense. Tears never seemed to run out, the pain wouldn't subside, but still I continued pushing myself to face each new morning because it was one closer to seeing him again. Right or wrong, that was my focus; get my life over with to bring me closer to the end where he'd be waiting.

During this time, I was at the cemetery every day without fail. Sometimes I would go twice, once in the morning and then again in the evening. There were times when I'd have company and I'd have to cut their visit short because I needed to get to the cemetery before dark. I distinctly remember feeling almost panicked inside because the sun was starting to go down and the person hadn't left yet. Finally, I came right out and said I had to get to there while it was still light out.

I kept a small folding stool in my trunk and I would sit by his grave talking, crying, and allowing myself to feel whatever emotions were present at the time. The plot he was buried in was chosen by me. After his funeral arrangements were made, I went to the cemetery with the family to make a location decision. We were brought to the section where he'd be laid to rest and the caretaker showed us a diagram of what was available. There was one directly at the end of the section which meant they would never be able to place any remains to Tyger's left. His would always be last in that row.

As soon as I heard that, I said, "That's the one. Whenever we'd go to the movies he liked the end seat in the row because I would be on one side of him and no one would be able to sit on the other. He never liked feeling surrounded, so the end spot is the right one."

On my visits, I would always place my stool on that side. Even though the plot on his right was vacant, someday it wouldn't be so I decided that side would be where I sat.

I spent so much of my time there that I became familiar with the man who cut the grass. He would wave when he saw me and sometimes we would speak. I told him how surprised I was at how quickly the grass was growing over Tyger's burial site and he explained how well-fertilized the ground is and what good drainage there was in that section. He let me know when it was time to cut the grass above his grave, or when Tyger would receive "his first haircut," as he put it. I was thankful for the information and to know the man took pride in his job. He respected those who were laid to rest.

Although I knew in my heart that Tyger wasn't there and it was simply the resting place of his remains, I had to be there. It was the last place I knew he had been physically and, quite honestly, I didn't know where else to go. I needed a place to visit with him and this was it now.

As unbelievable as it was, this was where I spent my evenings. The time that had once belonged to us when we would catch up on the day's activities or lay in each other's arms in front of the TV. This was the way I now spent "our time," sitting by his grave with a broken heart. My life consisted of missing him and clinging to the love he left me with.

It took nearly two weeks before I had the courage to see Sophia. I was terrified of how I'd feel when I saw the little girl. The three of us had spent so much time together and made so many happy memories. How would I be able to look at her and not completely fall apart? Not only that, but I knew she would have questions I probably wouldn't be able to answer. Her mother had told her about Tyger's passing and she said Sophia took it pretty well. I knew it would be different once she saw me, though.

At last, I gathered the strength to go and get her. She was happy to see me and seemed to be her usual talkative self. I found it odd that she didn't mention Mike, not even once.

After a while, I asked, "Soph, do you know Mike died?"

She looked up at me nervously and said, "Yes, but Mommy told me not to talk about Mike because it would make you sad."

I told her it was all right, she could talk about him. As soon as I said those words, she burst into the saddest, most heartbreaking tears I'd ever heard. This precious, little, five-year-old had been trying to be strong for me while she was in pain herself. I did the only thing I could do which was to hold her in my arms and cry with her.

In the moments that followed, we wept for this man who had touched our hearts so deeply and for the tomorrows that would never be.

After a while, she asked, "Nani, why did Mike die?"

I tried to answer in a way she could understand, so I said, "His heart was sick and it stopped working."

She was quiet for a minute and then asked, "Can we get him a new heart so he can come back?"

"No, honey, we can't do that, but Mike will always be with us because he lives in *our* hearts. He loves us and we love him and we can remember all the fun times we had together. We can talk about him and remember him all the time."

She seemed comforted by that, yet still so very sad.

When I spoke to her mother later, I thanked her for trying to spare my feelings, but explained it was important to let Sophia express what she was feeling.

As time went on, Sophia would play a pivotal role on my path to healing. She and I share memories of Tyger that no one else has. Like when they'd tickle each other's necks, laugh so hard, and then he'd say, "Soph, one more time. Get me again," and she would do it every time. There was the day I was picking her up from preschool and he called to see if she'd like a donut. We met him at Dunkin Donuts and he bought Sophie her favorite chocolate munchkins. They were mostly quick visits, but those few moments meant so much. Also, the way she'd hide from him—always in the same exact place—when he knocked at the door. He'd walk in and pretend not to know where she was and then say he was leaving since she wasn't there. She would pop out, giggling, and run to him every single time. The times we would take her out for French fries and ice cream which were two of her favorites. She'd always eat all her fries and then help him finish his. The trinkets she would bring in her backpack whenever we went to his place to visit and his interest when she showed him what she'd brought.

The three of us experienced so much together and made such wonderful memories. I would soon learn how badly I needed to keep her close and how important it was for both her and me. The more she spoke about him, the more I realized she would never, ever forget her Mikey.

Neither would I.

CHAPTER FOUR
Lessons in Self Love

"SO, WHEN DO YOU TAKE the time to do anything for yourself?"

This was a question Tyger asked me when we were getting to know each other.

I paused and thought for a moment, but I really couldn't answer.

He said, "You're always talking about what you did around the house or the things you do for your kids, but you never mention anything about doing things you enjoy. When do you have Diane time?"

Wow, was he seriously asking this? Never in my life had anyone made me stop to even consider doing something just for me. He forced me to take a good, long look at myself and figure out exactly what it was I might enjoy doing. I supposed in the hectic pace of life it had never occurred to me that I deserved to take time out for myself.

From Tyger's perspective, I was a hard worker, focused on taking care of home and all my family obligations, yet I never stopped to do anything simply because I enjoyed it.

He said to me, "Every once in a while, it's important for you to just do, Diane."

Even though I'd never considered it, he made a lot of sense.

I began to do little things just for me. A bus trip to New York City to do some sight-seeing. Random shopping trips which ended in buying items I didn't necessarily need, but really wanted. Going for the occasional manicure and pedicure. Once or twice I even went to Victoria's Secret and bought some sexy lingerie. That was huge for me because most of my undergarments came in multi-packs from a department store.

I soon realized the more I did for myself, the more tolerant I became of the tedious day-to-day activities. It didn't always involve spending money either. Sometimes it was something as simple as listening to my iPod as I walked around the park, or packing a lunch and heading to the beach for the day. It was "Diane time" and it enhanced my life in ways I never knew I needed. It was all thanks to this wonderful man who called my attention to what was missing.

He loved to tell me how long he'd been an admirer of mine. "I've had my eye on you for the past ten years," he said.

Long before we'd ever had our first conversation, he was attracted to me and interested in getting to know me. Of course, being my usual naive self, I hadn't suspected anything. He told me about the times at work when he'd watch me walk across the street in my white lab coat until I disappeared from view. Again,

I had no clue of any of this. He spoke of how beautiful he thought I was and the look in his eyes confirmed every word he was saying. In our early conversations, he asked for a picture of me. When I asked why he wanted one, he said, "So I can have it blown up, hang it on my wall, and enjoy your beauty."

Of course, I laughed it off because there was no way he'd really do that.

Once we became more than friends I gave him a picture. A few weeks later, I stopped by his place and on the couch sat a framed, poster-sized picture of me. I couldn't believe it, but there it was waiting to be hung on the wall.

My response was, "You have got to be kidding me."

He said, "You thought I was playing? Next time you go by the photo section at Walmart, don't be surprised if the lady recognizes you. She was impressed I was having this done and asked me to come back to tell her how you reacted when you saw it."

He turned his old bedroom into his "Diane room." At least, that was what he called it. He put his stereo in there and a few decorative pieces. On the wall was that huge picture of me and later he also hung a framed poem I'd written for him as a gift. Was I dreaming? No, I was wide awake and these beautiful things were really happening.

It's important to stop and explain a bit more about the type of man Tyger was. This wasn't a weak-minded, led-around-by-the-nose type of guy. He was all man; the kind who put the "m" in masculine. A true force to be reckoned with and, although he was a great person, you did *not* want to get on his bad side. He never went looking for trouble, but he sure knew what to do if it should happen to find him. He had his opinions of right and wrong and didn't hesitate to share them regardless of what anyone else might think. I refer back to his size—well above average at six-foot-five and over 400 pounds—so when he spoke, people listened. He was a true leader in his circle of friends and a man who others looked up to. He was someone who did things for one reason and one reason only: because he wanted to.

This wasn't a guy you'd shake your head about because he was under the spell of some female. Make no mistake about it, he was all man. His character made everything he was saying to and doing for me all the more special. This was out of the norm for him, yet he was doing these things willingly and genuinely enjoying it. I often called him my "real man." He was hard when he had to be and gentle when it mattered.

I've always been an independent person and never had patience with women who played the helpless role or behaved like they needed a man to save them. I was in relationships in my past where I had to basically fill both roles because the man in my life wasn't exactly pulling his weight. Yet now, I was experiencing something totally unlike anything I'd known before. I was with a guy who was not only comfortable, but extremely capable in his role of the male half of "us." It was a wonderful feeling to know I didn't have to go it alone and someone truly "had my back" in every situation.

One day, I was telling him my next door neighbors were cleaning out an apartment and were throwing old furniture and junk out on the sidewalk. The problem was instead of putting it in front of their house it was practically in front of mine.

I said to Tyger, "These people need to keep their junk in front of their own house. Why do I have to look like I belong on an episode of *Sanford and Son*?"

He sort of laughed, but didn't really comment. The next time he came over, I saw him pull up, but after several minutes, he still hadn't come in. I looked out the window and there he was throwing all their junk back in front of their house. All I could do was laugh. He hadn't even hinted at it bothering him when I complained about it and never in my wildest dreams did I expect him to do that, but he sure was. I guess the fact that it bothered me bothered him and he was not having it.

I have to mention again how much of our time we spent laughing together. There was a lot to be said for the ability to make another person laugh and we certainly had that effect on one another.

He was the type of person who liked to be aware of his surroundings, so he paid attention to the goings-on in his neighborhood. At the same time, he wasn't fond of people keeping up with what *he* was doing, so it was a delicate balance of watching out for the neighbors, but staying below the radar himself.

We were laying on his bed one night talking and he told me about his neighbors: the man across the street had dropped off a load of mulch, the people in the white house with their "bad-assed kids," the old lady on the corner had been taken away by ambulance again, and those people in the blue house who were forever looking out their window.

So, I said to him, "Oh, really? They're always in the window, huh?"

He said, "Yeah, they are some nosey people, either that or they're peeking out the front door."

I thought about it for a second and then said, "Well, how would you know they're looking out unless you're doing the same thing from over here?"

I burst out laughing and he said, "That's it... turn around. I don't even wanna see you right now." He laughed all the while as he said it. That was always his reaction when I called him out on something.

As the chuckling continued, I'd usually get what we called "the hand to the face," which was one of his giant hands completely covering my face in an attempt to make me stop laughing. That only made me laugh harder.

Another time, he shared with me how he didn't like his upstairs neighbors seeing what bags he was bringing in from the store, so he'd try to conceal them as he walked across the yard to his door.

I said to him, "You really think they're sitting up there by the window waiting for you to pull up so they can see the bags you're carrying? Is one of them perched there as a lookout and when you get home he yells to the other one, "Here he comes! Let's see what bags he's carrying"?

His response was, "Well, when you put it like that it sounds ridiculous."

I said, "Oh, coming from me it sounds ridiculous, but you tip-toeing through the yard like a secret squirrel is perfectly normal."

We were so completely comfortable with each other we could share any and everything. We laughed at the silly things we did because we were able to always relax and completely be ourselves. He had a habit of parking in the emptiest area of whatever parking lot he was in because he didn't like other cars too close to him. One day, I was driving through town and I noticed his car at the auto parts store. Sure enough, it was at the far end of the lot, sitting all by itself. I pulled in right next to it and waited for him to come out. He walked out of the store and when he looked in the direction of his vehicle, he stopped in his tracks. I sat there laughing to myself because I knew what he was thinking: *Why the hell is that car right next to mine? All these empty spaces and they had to park right next to me?*

He started walking across the lot and when he was close I got out laughing. I told him I knew what he was thinking when he saw a car so close to his and I'd done that on purpose. Once he realized it was me, he relaxed and saw the humor in it, but he was highly agitated when he first stepped out and noticed a car there. It didn't even occur to him it could be me, he just couldn't get over the fact that someone had parked right next to him.

I was leaving his house one night around 11:00 p.m. or so. It was dark out and his driveway was at the far end of the yard. He would always stand at the door and watch to make sure I got to my car safely. This particular night, we noticed there was a small pick-up truck in the road blocking his driveway. We could see the driver's side door was open, although there didn't seem to be anyone around.

Tyger says, "Wait here in the kitchen. I'll be right back."

He went into his bedroom and came back carrying a baseball bat. He calmly said, "Let's go check this out."

We crossed the yard. Just as we got to the truck, a young guy in his early twenties came running up the hill. Tyger calmly stood there with the bat concealed at his side and asked, "Is this your truck?"

The young man, obviously nervous, said, "Yes, sir. My friend took my truck without my permission and it's a stick-shift and he really didn't know how to drive it. He knew I'd be pissed, so he took off and left it. I'm sorry, sir, I'm really sorry for the inconvenience. I don't know where he went."

After listening to this young man ramble on and on, my honey simply said to him, "My man, can you just move the truck?"

The guy jumped in the driver's seat and was gone in seconds.

I said to him, "Really, baby? You didn't think your size was enough? Did you really need the bat, too?"

His answer was something I'll never forget. He said, "The worst mistake anyone can make is to underestimate another person. You never know what they're capable of regardless of their size. The cemeteries are full of big guys who underestimated the little guy."

I realized how right he was.

Tyger was my knight in shining armor, always a phone call away. One night on my way home from work, I started having car trouble. I pressed on the gas pedal, but the car kept going slower and slower and all the lights on the dash started flashing. I managed to get to the side of the road before it came to a complete stop. I tried to restart it, but nothing happened.

There I was at 11:00 p.m. on this dark road scared to death. I called my love and woke him up.

He listened and then said, "I'm on my way."

When he got there, he went to grab his jumper cables and realized he didn't have them. He said to me, "C'mon, we're going to Walmart."

Off we went to the twenty-four-hour Walmart Super Center and he bought two sets of cables; one for him and one for me. He was able to get my car started, but it died again a short way up the road. We got permission to leave it in a gas station parking lot. We drove back to his house and he had me take his SUV home since he had two vehicles.

The next day, while I was at work, he and some mechanic friends figured out the problem was my alternator. He had them replace it and also picked up a new battery since the bad alternator had completely drained it. My car was back on the road in no time and I was so grateful to have someone in my life who knew exactly how to get things done.

Several months later, I took Markie and Sophia out to dinner. On our way home, a deer came out of nowhere and ran directly into the front driver's side of my car. It literally ran into us. One minute we were talking and laughing and the next it was sheer chaos. Brakes squealing, air bags deployed, everyone screaming—it was terrifying.

When we came to a stop on the side of the road, I checked my son and granddaughter to make sure neither was hurt. Thankfully, they were fine, just quite shaken up. As far as I could tell, I wasn't hurt either, but the front end was a wreck. The hood was completely bent, the radiator was pushed back, and the impact had caused the stereo inside the car to be pushed out. The windshield was cracked because the deer had rolled up on the hood. Inside the car, we were choking on the powder in the air that came from the deployment of the airbags.

I cleared my mind enough to open the windows. I was so relieved to see a volunteer fireman who'd been coming from the opposite direction as the accident happened. He stopped and ran over to check on us and then directed traffic. I dialed 911 and the state police were dispatched.

My next call was to Tyger and, once again, his response was, "I'm on my way."

Sophia was scared and crying, so Markie found some cartoons on his phone and gave it to her as a distraction. The deer was hurt badly and laying in the grass off to the far right. We didn't want Sophia to see it.

She asked, "Nani, why did you hit Santa's reindeer? Where did he go?"

I told her, "It was an accident, baby. Nani didn't mean it. He went back into the woods to be with his family."

When Tyger got there, he strolled over to the car and said, "Hey, what are you guys doing?" He was calm, like it was a bright, sunny afternoon. We were all in shock and hadn't even thought about getting out of the wreckage.

As soon as Sophia saw him, she started to cry and said, "Mike, Nani hit Santa's reindeer and I'm scared."

He opened the back door, got her out of her car seat, and carried her to his car talking to her the whole way, asking what she was watching on Markie's phone and trying to get her mind off what had happened. The state police had shown up by then and needed to put the deer down. They didn't want to do that in front of the kids.

Tyger said, "Take the kids home in my car. I'll stay here and wait for the tow truck."

I did that and Markie watched Sophia while I went back to see about my car. After it had been towed, Tyger gave me his SUV to use until my insurance company set me up with a rental.

His demeanor when he arrived at the scene of the accident had changed the entire atmosphere. I was shaking like a leaf and the kids were scared, but because Tyger was so calm and behaving like everything was normal, it calmed us down, as well. Once again, he saved the day and he did it willingly.

Having a man in my life who was always willing to step up and take the lead when necessary was a completely new experience. Even for an independent woman like me, it was a comforting feeling to know Tyger was always there and knew exactly what to do.

Following the accident with the deer, it took a while before I found the car I wanted and it cost a smidgen more than what I'd gotten from the insurance company. The owner of the garage where I was buying it was willing to hold the car for a couple of weeks until I had the full amount. In the meantime, I had to give the rental back so Tyger told me I could drive his Cadillac until I got my car. He said he needed his SUV, so I'd have to take the Caddy. To say I was nervous about driving his pride and joy would be an understatement. I fully expected a long list of dos and don'ts from him, but instead, all he said to me was, "Don't be driving my car like no wimp."

It didn't take long before I was very comfortable with that beautiful machine. I enjoyed the power under the hood and I'd tell him how fun it was to drive. It was a bigger vehicle than I was used to, but it was such a nice riding car and definitely an attention grabber. The fact that he trusted me enough to hand over the keys was a wonderful feeling.

More than once during the time I had it, I would get in to leave for work in the morning to find the tank was full. It hadn't been that way when I'd parked it the night before, yet in the morning it was. Tyger would come by at night, park his SUV, take the Caddy and fill the tank, then bring it back and go home without saying a word. Not only was he letting me drive his car, he was also supplying the gas.

When I mentioned to him I didn't expect him to do that and fully intended to put gas in the car since I was driving it, he simply smiled and said not to worry about it.

Never in my life had I felt so well-cared for.

He said to me once, "You make me want to do better. I never want to do anything that would make people wonder what you see in me."

He was conscious of his actions and how they could be perceived. In his words, he "stepped his game up" at work, as well, paying even more attention to the quality of what he did. His willingness to share so much with me made it so easy for me to open up to him about everything. There was never a sense of judgment or a fear we might think less of one another no matter what was said. What a comforting feeling it was to relax and just be ourselves.

Many times, I said to him, "You are a rare find."

He was quick to respond that he hadn't always been this way and there were women in his past who'd have a hard time believing he was even capable of the level of attention he was showing me. The dynamic of our relationship and treatment of each other was a completely new to both of us. As surprised as I was to be so well cared-for, he was equally surprised that I'd never experienced this before.

We didn't realize it at the time, but we were actually teaching each other what it meant to give love selflessly and receive it wholeheartedly. In the process, we were boosting the level of self-confidence and self-esteem in one another. It was never about impressing other people or an attempt at living up to someone else's relationship standards. It was always about doing what felt right for *us* by doing what we wanted without any distractions.

These are observations I've made in hindsight because while it was going on, we were living in the moment. No pressure, no analyzing, no preconceived notions. There was only pure pleasure. We enjoyed making each other happy and we were quite good at it.

As time went on, I noticed I didn't second guess myself the way I had in the past and I held my head higher when I walked. What others thought of me didn't matter one bit because I was loved, appreciated, and secure in who I was. The smile that had become a permanent fixture on my face came from a place deep within that no one had ever been able to reach before.

One night, he said to me, "From now, on whenever I ask who the most beautiful girl in the world is, I want you to answer, 'I am.'"

This became a regular thing for us and every time I answered, he'd say, "That's right. You are."

All this was changing me from the inside out and taking our love to a whole other level.

For most of my adult life, I've struggled with my weight. Not that I've ever been extremely overweight, but the battle of the bulge was something I knew well and it only got worse after age forty. Tyger never complained one bit regardless of what I weighed, even those times when I felt heavier than I was comfortable with.

He'd say, "Those few pounds ain't hurting anybody. That's just goodness."

I'd diet and exercise and lose the pounds anyway, but he was happy either way. The look in his eyes never changed no matter what size I was or how my hair looked or what I was wearing or whether or not I had on make-up.

He used to say, "You could show up wearing a burlap potato sack and still look great to me."

I was sure he meant it. His words and actions taught me how to see the good in myself. He was proud to call me his girl and I was so pleased he was my man. We were two people who came together and built each other up in so many ways.

As amazing as our relationship was, it wasn't without the occasional hiccups. Although they were few and far between, we disagreed a time or two and reacted in completely opposite ways. When something upset him, his response was to withdraw and completely shut down. He hadn't always been that way. He shared plenty of stories about how in his younger days, his temper could be explosive if provoked. This had landed him in trouble more than once and after many years of paying the price for that behavior, he had learned that removing himself in order to cool off was the best way of handling things. This drove me absolutely out of my mind because I would've preferred talking out whatever had caused the disagreement or even exchanging some loud words so we could put it behind us. It was impossible to do that though because when he shut down, he shut all the way down. That meant he wouldn't answer the phone or reply to texts until he was good and ready.

During this time, I'd tell myself: *That's it. If he doesn't want to talk to me, then I don't want to talk to him. When he calls I'm telling him it's over.* After a day or two, he'd call or text and we'd pick up right where we'd left off before the incident and then move forward. Cooler heads always prevailed.

We were able to do this because the good in what we had far outweighed the bad. The happiness we brought to each other's lives was more than enough reason to get past the occasional misunderstood words or overreaction to something that was said.

Once things were back to normal, I'd remark that I thought he was through with me. His answer was, "I'd have to be a damn fool to ever lose you. I'm far from a fool."

He called me his "dream girl" and he was the man of my dreams. He showered me with so much attention and never left a doubt in my mind as to how he felt about me. He had so many names for me: his *cherry on top*, his *over-the-top-wow-girl*, his *pretty baby.* Never in my life had I ever felt so completely adored and I felt the same way about him. As much time as he spent paying me compliments, hearing praise about himself made him uncomfortable. I didn't stop though because I enjoyed seeing him squirm. He obviously liked hearing the nice things I said, but he was never sure how to react.

Once, we were in the car and he was driving. I looked over and said, "I love your eyes. You have amazing eyes. What color are they?"

He had dark eyes outlined with a grayish color, just beautiful.

Another time I said, "You have such nice lips. I love kissing them."

His reaction was the same every time which was to pretend he hadn't heard me and quickly change the subject. Even though he didn't respond, he knew I meant every word and how proud I was to call him my man. In the process of loving each other, we were also learning how to love ourselves and it was a beautiful thing.

CHAPTER FIVE
Dual Transformation

CHANGE IS GOOD. I'd been told that all my life, but I never once believed it. I preferred the tried and true and the "keep things as they are" approach. Or, at least, I always had until he walked into my world.

There's something about feeling completely loved that gives you the courage to step out on faith. That was why when I received the news that my job of twenty years would soon be coming to an end, it didn't sound as terrifying as it may have at another stage in my life. I was definitely knocked back a few steps when I heard the news, but after some thought and serious soul searching, it was clear what I needed to do.

In March 2014, it was announced that the department I'd worked in was being outsourced to another company. We were basically given three options: 1) apply for a position with the new company, 2) apply for an open position within the casino, or 3) accept a severance package and leave the casino altogether. After twenty years of working in food service, I was burnt out and borderline miserable. I'd worked my way up to a management position, but I had never left the department I started in. Even still, my initial thought was I would apply for a management position with the new company. With my experience and good performance record, it seemed likely they'd hire me. Besides it was the *safe* thing to do.

I shared my plans with Tyger and he asked, "Are you sure that's what you want to do?"

"Yes," I answered. "I have to work to support myself so this is the only thing that makes sense."

Again, he asked, "Are you really sure? You know how unhappy you've been at work lately. This would be the same or worse, you know."

He was right and I knew it, but I was afraid to take a chance so it seemed like my only option. He had left the casino a few months earlier after twelve years there. His dream was to one day open a jazz club. A place that would cater to the "grown folk's crowd" where people could go and listen to good music. He wanted to have a kitchen and offer a light menu. With my food service/management background, I would be able to help with that. He also wanted me to take care of the office work. I enjoyed administrative duties anyway and always gravitated toward the office responsibilities even in my current position, so it was something he was confident I could handle. In the meantime, he had started a production company, promoting local artists and giving them a venue where they could showcase their talent.

He began organizing events geared toward an older crowd with music and dancing in line with the idea for his future jazz club. He would rent a hall and I'd help with set up, decorating, making centerpieces for the tables, and small details. He was the visionary, though, and the creative genius behind the entire production. His ideas and attention to detail were second to none and he knew how to turn his concepts into reality. He positioned the right people in the right places to make his plans come to life and he had a hand in every single step. At one of his most successful events called "The After Nine Affair," he had a large poster printed with my picture on it which read, "Lady D. Presents the After Nine Affair."

Two days before the event, he showed it to me and said, "This will be at the door as people come in."

Having been a modest, shy person my entire life, I said to him, "What? You can't put that at the door."

"Oh, yes, I can," he said. "This will be the first thing they see because you are the face of the business."

Despite my initial reaction, how could this gesture make me feel anything but confident? It was a totally new experience for me being treated this way and it felt great.

After a few days of wrestling with the decision of whether or not to apply for a job with the new company, I decided to pray about it. I asked God if I was doing the right thing. Should I take a job, or accept the severance package, take some time off and completely reinvent myself? I laid there thinking about it and then I suddenly knew the answer: take this opportunity, step out on faith, and walk away.

As I finished this thought, I immediately felt an overwhelming sense of peace. It was the right decision.

The next morning, I told Tyger about it and I could hear the happiness in his voice when he said, "That's my girl. Now you're making sense."

"Yes," I said. "I'm taking the summer off to enjoy myself, I deserve it after twenty years of hard work. When I'm ready, maybe I'll take some classes and apply at a medical office to do billing and coding."

He liked the sound of that, especially the time off part.

He was the inspiration behind my making that life changing decision. The old me never would've had the courage to take a risk like that, but I felt so loved and so safe and protected by that love that I knew right down to my core I would never completely fall. Oh, sure, there would be bumps in the road now and then, but fall? Never. Not as long as I had his love and his belief in me. We had that effect on one another.

When we first started out, he made it clear to me that he did not do relationships. We could see each other and enjoy it for however long it lasted, but he wasn't looking for anything long term. I was actually fine with that. We were having fun and we were happy. Why complicate things by labeling it or pressuring each other into giving more than we could? It felt right, it felt *good,* so why not relax and let things happen? That was exactly what we were doing, but over time, we each began to crave more of that happiness. He continued to speak the same words, no relationships or anything long term, but his actions didn't match. Our time together grew and he began opening up about of himself. I was willing to accept things however he wanted them and our bond kept getting stronger. We were both very independent people who believed deeply in being self-sufficient. We each appreciated having our own space and occasional alone time, but we also cherished our time together. We had balance and it worked. No one was talking about living together. There didn't seem to be a need. We were completely in love and incredibly happy. Two individuals who did well on their own, but were even better together.

His influence on my life improved everything. I had always been the shy, quiet type. I never liked to make waves or cause friction. He taught me it was okay to stand up for myself. Thinking back to the early stages of our relationship, I'd tell him about someone upsetting me. He'd ask what I'd said in return and my usual response would be, "I didn't say anything. I don't care. Whatever."

He'd say, "No, not whatever. Stop using that word 'whatever.' I hate it. You need to speak up and stop laying down like a doormat."

My initial reaction was, "I'm not a doormat," but as I thought about it, he was right.

Why did I feel it was acceptable for someone to say something I didn't like that would upset *me?* Why did I shrug it off because I was worried about upsetting *them?* What gave them more of a right to express their thoughts than I had? Nothing, that's what. I learned to speak up about things I didn't agree with rather than suffer in silence. It wasn't long before I realized how much better this made me feel. Tyger's love empowered me and gave me the courage to express myself and voice my opinions. He was very protective of me, never wanting to see me taken advantage of in any way by anyone. His approach was always nurturing and never overbearing. He would question why I allowed certain things to go on and why I felt comfortable complaining to him, yet not addressing the situation. The things I was unhappy about were minor conflicts, work issues, or sometimes family problems. Had it been anything major, he would've instantly gone into defense mode. He taught me how to stand on my own two feet and it was a lesson I'd never forget.

He opened up to me about so many things. I loved hearing stories about his childhood and what it had been like being part of such a large family. To an only child like myself, that sounded so exciting, but he would tell me I was the one who had it good growing up. Even having said that, he had many wonderful memories to share. Sometimes he'd start telling me about something, then say, "Damn it, I told myself I wasn't gonna tell you that." I'd say, "Too late. Spit it out."

Most of these conversations took place while we were in his bed. Sometimes right in the middle of a story, he'd start to doze off. After a second or two, he'd wake up and continue with the next word he was about to say without missing a beat.

I would ask, "How do you do that??" He'd deny ever having fallen asleep, then tell me to, "Roll the tape, run that back so I can see if I fell asleep or not."

He shared so much with me about past relationships and how after some pretty bad experiences he'd made it a practice not to let any woman get too close. He liked to keep it casual and if he felt they became too attached or demanded a lot of his time, he would distance himself. He enjoyed the freedom of not really being tied down.

We had started out that way, but evolved into something greater. He said he found himself in unfamiliar territory with me; enjoying our time together and before he knew it, he had fallen in love. This was a new experience for me, as well. In my past relationships, I had always been the one who wanted to move in together, to take the next step. With Tyger, I didn't feel the need to do that. We were living well, each in our own space, and it made us appreciate our "together time" even more.

So often, I would say to him, "I love my life. I love the way I'm living."

He was always happy to hear that and to know he had contributed to my new way of living and embracing life. I told him once that it felt as though I'd been stumbling around in the dark before he came into my world. I finally knew who I was and what I wanted for the first time ever. He said the same was true for him.

Life was very good.

He was the first to mention love in our relationship.

We were talking about us and all of a sudden he told me about the moment he knew he was in love with me. I was surprised by this because of how adamant he'd been in the beginning of not wanting anything serious.

When I responded and said I loved him, as well, his response was, "You do? Why?"

I said, "Because you make me happier than I've ever been in my entire life. You treat me like every day is our first day together."

He listened quietly, but I could tell he wasn't sure he could believe me. It was as if in his mind it couldn't possibly be true.

He even asked me once, "How can someone like you love someone like me?"

I wasn't sure what he meant by that, so I assumed he was referring to his past and how he'd lived. I told him that had nothing to do with anything now. I respected him so much for what he shared with me. It spoke to the character of the man he had become. A person of integrity who was willing to lay his cards on the table and leave himself exposed. A man who didn't hide from anything and made me feel completely safe, protected, and loved. How could I possibly *not* fall in love with him for all those reasons? After some time, he came to believe in my love for him.

I would say, "I love you," and he'd answer, "I know you do."

Tyger's apartment was at the top of a huge hill which was a nightmare to deal with in the winter. After living there a few years, he decided it was time to move. He was able to find a place he really liked and was excited to show it to me. We walked from room to room as he described his ideas for what would go where. He asked me to decorate his kitchen and bathroom because he wanted my involvement so it would feel like my place, too. I was surprised by that since I knew he had excellent taste and he could definitely handle it himself. My mind was already working on ideas of what to do in each room. We had so much fun decorating and getting things in order. I went shopping for curtains and other items for the bathroom.

He joked about how his oldest sister and I both had "fluffy bathrooms" and he wanted one, too. So, I went all out with it coordinating everything right down to the fancy towels.

He asked if he was supposed to use them and I said, "No, use your old towels when you shower. These are just for show."

He thought that was crazy, but he followed the rule anyway.

The bathroom was nicely done; decorative, yet still masculine. We went to the store together to pick out pictures for the bathroom and kitchen walls. He was very happy with the end result in both rooms. His plan worked perfectly, too, because it definitely felt like home to me since I'd been so involved.

As he set up the remaining rooms, he'd call and say, "You have to come see this. Wait until you see what I did."

I'd be excited to get there to check out his handiwork and I'd be blown away every time. There were days we'd be getting the place together and he'd have to leave for something. I'd stay and continue with whatever I was doing and still be busy when he got back. The whole process was natural to both of us even though it was so far from anything he'd done in previous relationships. I was given access to areas of his life that he hadn't allowed anyone to enter in the past. He said with me, it was different and it just, "felt right."

Some days, I'd have Sophia with me and she'd be busy drawing pictures for him or playing his keyboard while I hung curtains or pictures. The two of them would entertain each other while I got things done. It was great because she was a distraction from all the work I was doing. He loved to tell me I was doing too much or that was enough for today. My method of operation has always been I need everything done yesterday and breaks are an unnecessary waste of time. With Soph there, he was busy with her and I was able to get lots done without him bugging me about working too hard. It was a winning situation for all of us.

So, this man who had once said he didn't do relationships found himself in a serious one and he was extremely happy about it. When he started getting comfortable with how to use Facebook, he posted about his girl or his "squeeze," as he sometimes called me. He constantly shared pictures of us. This extremely private guy who let few people get close to him was opening up. He was happy, in love, and well-loved in return and he wanted the world to know it.

I asked him once, "What had happened to change your mind about relationships?"

In the beginning, he'd talked about his "rule book" which wasn't an actual book, but his philosophy on interacting with women. With me, though, he became more concerned with my happiness which caused him to tear page after page out of this "rule book."

There was a day we'd been out for quite a while and then he asked if I wanted to go for coffee. I told him I didn't want to take up any more of his time and he said, "You never take up my time because, with you, it's different. You, I *like*." That was a reference to what he'd told me about women he'd been with in the past and how he'd made excuses to limit his time with them. "I enjoy you" was something he said to me often.

We began attending family events, both his and mine. People couldn't help but notice how happy we were and the word I heard most often when describing us was "glowing." We both had a glow when we were together. I was told constantly how enjoyable my daily Facebook posts were. Everything was so positive and it was nice to see someone so happy.

One day, we were out for a ride and he said, "I want you to have a key to my place."

I answered with a simple, "Okay, baby." However, I could hardly believe my ears.

We stopped at a hardware store, he made a copy of the key, and then he handed it to me. It wasn't just having the key that impressed me, it was the message that came along with it. This was a huge statement of trust and it meant everything to me. We'd come a long way in over three years. It all developed slowly and naturally. We fell in love over time without pressuring each other about anything. We'd both been married twice—his two children were adults and I had one adult son with my youngest in high school. There were no little ones to consider, so we had the freedom to do as we pleased. Neither of us expressed any desire to marry again although anything was possible. We were taking life as it came and it was all good.

He spoke about buying a house one day and said, "I want to buy a duplex. I'll live on one side and you can live on the other." Most people might find that strange, but it really would've worked for us.

My last day at the casino was June 1, 2014. It was bittersweet, for sure, as I looked forward to the future, but I would miss the people I considered friends.

One of the first things I did with my newly acquired free time was to buy a season parking pass to a local beach. This was my summer off and I was planning to be an official beach bum. Tyger loved the fact that I was doing what I enjoyed. I'd text him from my spot on the sand or send pictures of Sophia playing in the water. Since his place was on the way, we would stop to see him on our way to the beach. I'd pull up out front and text him to step outside. He'd come out and say a few words to Sophia. Other times, we'd run in for a minute to say a quick hello. If he wasn't home, we'd stop to see him on our way back and tell him about our day in the sun.

On the weekdays, it was "Diane time" and I'd head off to the beach alone. During that time, I would put my headphones on and listen to music; soaking up the sun without having to keep a constant watch on a little one. I enjoyed myself either way and on the drive home, I was always excited about whatever plans Tyger and I had for later. Even if those plans were only to speak on the phone and discuss what we were watching on TV, I looked forward to it.

Summer was off to a great start. Tyger was busy getting new sound equipment for the production company and planning upcoming events. His best friend was a partner in the business and Tyger's nephew was involved as well. They were organizing a large, outdoor event to be held in August so he had a lot going on. This didn't mean we missed out on any time together, though. We continued going out to eat or taking nice long rides to nowhere in particular. There was always our "alone time," as well, which was the best of all. I adjusted quickly to not having to get up for work considering it was the first time in two decades I was without a job. The highlight of every morning was opening my eyes, reaching for the phone, calling Tyger, and hearing his voice when he answered.

June seemed to fly right by and July moved fast, as well. My family reunion was being held on July 19 and he was going with me for the first time. He knew many of my family members since we'd grown up in the same town, but the reunion was in Rhode Island so he met even more of my family. What a great day it was.

Tyger had been best friends with one of my cousins when they were boys and the two of them had the best time catching up and reminiscing. Every year, we have what we call "family circle." We gather our chairs around a big tree and everyone gets up and say a few words to the family about anything at all they'd like to share. I introduced Tyger as "my man," so overjoyed to have him there with me.

We took lots of pictures and spent the day talking, laughing, eating, and enjoying ourselves. When he saw how nice the pictures of the two of us were, he had me enlarge some and make copies. He wanted to give his sisters the bigger ones and the smaller ones to friends.

In the days that followed, he would text me every time he handed out another picture of us. This was an absolute first for him as he had spent the majority of his life keeping his relationship status completely private. Yet, there he was, sharing photos of us and it had all been his idea.

I began thinking about his birthday that was fast approaching on July 30th. It was going to be a day I'd never forget. One that would send me plummeting from my seat on top of the world.

CHAPTER SIX
The Long, Hard Fall

IT IS ABSOLUTELY TERRIFYING when you feel like a stranger in your own life.

One minute you're completely comfortable and the next you don't recognize a single thing. Whose life is this anyway? Surely, it can't be mine.

Yet, this was my life, or, at least, what was left of it.

It consisted of non-stop tears and deep, agonizing pain. An ache and longing that went beyond my heart and was coming from the depths of my soul. It was impossible for me to make sense of anything. How could he have just disappeared? He was my "every day."

The first thing I did every morning was I called him and now I couldn't? I would never again wake up to a text he'd sent in the middle of the night?

I wandered around like a zombie for weeks. Sometimes, I'd get in the car and drive with no clue of where I was going. I didn't dare turn the radio on in case they played a song that reminded me of him. I'd end up at a store and go in to walk around. Right in the middle of an aisle. I'd ask myself, "What are you doing here?" I'd look at the people shopping and get so angry with them. How dare they talk and laugh like everything is normal? Don't they realize he's gone?

The intense pain was bad enough and then the anxiety attacks started. I'd be at the kitchen sink when an overwhelming fear would wash over me at the thought of not seeing him again, not hearing his voice, not going for a ride or out to eat. It was so bad that I would nearly hyperventilate and have to sit down for a while. Outwardly, I appeared to be functioning, but mentally and emotionally I was devastated.

Another cause of anxiety was the thought of living a long life. I was so afraid I'd live to be a ripe old age and it would take forever before I saw him again. So, I began asking God to let me die and to please end my life soon so I could be with my love. When I share this with people, they assume I contemplated suicide, but that wasn't the case. Never once did I consider taking my own life, I simply asked God to end it soon.

My mother passed away at age sixty-three, so my thinking was if I was lucky, I'd die fairly young, also. Since I'm in my late forties, living another fifteen years didn't seem long although I was really hoping to go sooner. I distinctly remember every time I felt the slightest twinge of pain in my body, I'd instantly say to myself, "Oh, good, maybe I'm sick. Maybe I have cancer or something."

I realize how terrible that sounds, especially coming from a mother and grandmother, but I was in unimaginable pain. I could not see the point in being here without Tyger and, quite honestly, I didn't want to be here. My main focus in those first weeks after he passed was to get the rest of my days over with as quickly as possible. I was still functioning as far as getting dressed, keeping the house somewhat in order, and going to the grocery store to have food in the house for my sons, but I had no intention of continuing on. One day, while shopping, I saw a multi-pack of paper towels on sale. I looked at it and thought to myself, "I won't need that many. I'm not going to live very long." It didn't seem wrong or strange to feel this way. It made perfect sense to me because my one and only goal was to be with Tyger again.

Posting things on Facebook as though I was speaking to him became an outlet for me. If I released the words into the atmosphere, they would reach him somehow. This gave me a way to vent and express what I was feeling. It helped for the most part, but what didn't help were the people who would say, "I know how you feel." Those words made me so angry. How dare they say that? No one knew how I felt. No one except Tyger and I knew the depth of our love or the importance of what we shared. It insulted me every time I heard those words. My pain was mine personally. It felt like an intrusion on something sacred and I vowed to never say that to anyone who was grieving a loss.

It also angered me when I'd say, "I miss him" and someone would say, "I miss him, too." Again, I was offended. Not because I doubted he was missed by many, but those other people still had their everyday routines intact. Maybe they missed seeing him around or speaking to him occasionally. For me, though, it was entirely different. He was like the air I breathed. There wasn't one day we didn't begin by speaking to each other. All day, every day we were texting or calling each other. Anytime the slightest thing happened, we instantly thought of sharing it with the other and usually did. I realize he had many friends and was loved so it didn't bother me when someone would say they missed him. What upset me was when they said it in response to my saying it, as though it was some sort of comparison or somehow equal in value. As I wrote these words, I realized how irrational it sounded, but at the time, I was anything but rational.

The evenings were extremely difficult and still are. That was our time when he'd either come by my place or I'd be at his. Now, all I did was sit on the couch, staring at the TV, not really watching, but I didn't know what else to do. To be honest, I there was nothing else I wanted to do. I wasn't looking to fill those hours or take my mind off of him. I longed for our "us time" back. If I couldn't have that, I didn't want anything.

Waking up in the morning was horrible, too. I'd lay there staring at my phone on the nightstand, thinking what I wouldn't give to pick it up and see a text from him. That could never happen, though. In fact, it would never ever happen again. More than once I seriously considered throwing the phone against the wall as hard as I could. The happiness I used to feel every time it rang or I heard a text notification was replaced by disgust because it would never be from him.

During this time, my family was trying so hard to include me in things. They would invite me to events, hoping to ease my mind even for a bit. I wasn't ready though and it got to a point where I had to ask them to please give me time. My heart couldn't handle large crowds of people enjoying themselves. I would be too aware of who was missing. The pain and sadness seemed to intensify when I saw people going about their lives because, for me, life seemed to be over. At least, the life I'd once recognized. The world was now a dark, unfamiliar place and I didn't feel as though I belonged in it.

I continued to experience a deep sense of guilt.

Why did I listen when he said he didn't want to go to the Emergency Room? How many minutes passed from when he first had trouble breathing to when he fell back on the porch? Would that have been enough time to get him to the hospital?

I asked myself these questions over and over and over again. I thought back to when he was first diagnosed with Congestive Heart Failure. It was about ten months earlier, he'd gotten up for work and was having trouble breathing. He had no idea what was happening since this was the first time he'd experienced it. He stood up and was trying to get air into his lungs. He said it felt like he was drowning, so he kept lifting his head higher as though he was trying to get above the water so he could breathe. He told me later he'd thought to himself, "Is this it? Is this how it feels when it's over and you're checking out?" After a few minutes, he was able to get enough air in to drive himself to the hospital. It wasn't until he didn't show up for work that I even knew something had happened. After calling him repeatedly, a nurse finally answered his cell phone and, with his permission, explained he was at the hospital but doing well.

As I replayed the night he passed away, I asked myself, "Was he afraid? Did he have those same thoughts again, wondering if this was the end?"

So many people tried to convince me I had no reason to feel guilty, but none of them were there. It was only Tyger and me and I loved him so much. I should have been able to save him. These hands of mine should have fixed the problem. It was my responsibility and I failed. Why didn't anyone else see it?

I had received a sympathy card from the Emergency Room staff where the doctor wrote, "Terribly sorry. Please know Michael did not suffer. Do not blame yourself."

I was the only other person there with him, though, so, of course, it was my fault. I'd let him down and this pain I was experiencing without him was my punishment for failing.

Somehow, I gathered the strength to go to his place and pack up his belongings. It had to be done and seemed fitting I should be the one to do it since we'd set it up together.

I paused in front of the built-in hutch in the dining room, thinking back to the day we'd cleaned the glass doors. He had taken care of the top row since he didn't need a step ladder to reach it. The sadness began welling up in me as I thought about how great that day had been, of our conversation, and the sheer enjoyment of simply being together. I took a deep breath and began removing the fancy dishes he had displayed in there. Memories of when he'd bought them and how pleased he was after setting them up were still fresh in my mind.

Next, I removed the battery-operated candles that had once created a warm glow on each shelf. Carefully, I wrapped each piece and packed them in a box.

In the bathroom, as I removed the curtains and pictures that hung on the walls, my mind replayed how pleased he was with how I'd decorated. When it was finished he'd asked me,

"Whose bathroom is this anyway? This is my bathroom?" I thought about the day I'd shown up with my iron and ironing board so I could press the new drapes. He'd said, "Just hang them up. They'll look fine." That wasn't how I did things, though, so I ironed them anyway. How could it be that I was now taking them down? We'd made so many memories in this home, so I took my time and packed everything neatly for whoever it would end up with.

As I went from room to room, I braced myself for what I might find. It wasn't like Tyger ever expected me to be going through his things, so it was possible I'd come across pictures of an ex-girlfriend or cards or letters he'd saved. I was prepared for that, but I found no such things. Not one picture, card, note, or anything else from another woman. What I did keep finding were pictures of me. He had recent photos in frames, but I found several more I'd given him over the years, tucked away in different drawers. Even though I knew how much he loved me, this seemed to validate it even more. I also came across his old cell phones. I smiled as I thought back to his philosophy every time he got a new one. He'd say, "I got you the same phone. Figure out how to use yours first, then you can teach me how to use mine."

Suddenly, I felt compelled to go through his old phones. It wasn't because I was searching for hidden secrets, our relationship hadn't been built on mistrust and we didn't go there with each other. This was different, though, and something was pushing me to do it. When I did, I was amazed at how many texts he had saved that were either to me or from me. He was never one to save texts, always deleting them as soon as he read them. So many times over the years, he'd start to show me something funny he'd received from someone and then wouldn't be able to find it. He'd say, "Damn it, I must've deleted it. I have a habit of deleting messages as soon as I read them." These hadn't been erased, though. They had meant something to him, so he'd locked them into his phone so he wouldn't get rid of them accidentally. Oh, how I cried when I found those. Even though I had no doubt of his love for me, this was such an amazing discovery and just another validation of his love.

Shortly after he passed, I was going through the calendar on his last phone, trying to figure out which of his bills were due when. I came across an entry he'd put in for April 2015 which said, "Start planning Diane's birthday bash in May." After my last birthday, he had told me he wanted to throw me a huge party for my next one.

His exact words were, "Everybody loves you, so they'll all come."

He only mentioned it that one time and we never spoke about it again.

Now, here I was looking at it in black and white. He'd really planned to go through with this. My heart was so touched and it brought more tears, but also a confirmation of his love for me.

I purposely left the bedroom for last. That was our space where we spent the most time together and shared our most intimate moments. When I finally gathered the courage to start packing things up in there, I simply collapsed on the bed and cried my eyes out. I was flooded with happy memories of lying there wrapped safely in his arms.

Slowly, I was able to begin packing his most personal items, including his clothes. I paused when I saw our slippers sitting side-by-side on the floor. A memory came back of him saying to me, "Why don't you leave some slippers here so you don't have to walk barefoot on these cold floors?" When I put my size seven slippers next to his size eighteen, we sat there laughing at the difference.

In the corner was a stool which was "my chair." We'd called it that because that was where I always put my clothes before laying down with him.

One day I said, "Hey, how come I always have to be naked, but you always get to keep something on?"

He said, "You just never mind that. I need to enjoy you. Trust me, if you lived here you'd be doing everything naked. Cooking, cleaning, everything."

Now, I stood staring at my chair, *how can any of this be real? That's my chair, where my clothes are supposed to go. Where are you, baby? I need you.*

So many tears and so much heartache as I slowly removed the pictures we'd hung together, one by one. As I think back to that day, I can still feel the pain in my chest and the sadness in my soul over never being able to enjoy each other the way we'd done so many times before.

I offered some of his clothing to his brothers and nephews, but because of his size, there really wasn't anyone who could wear them. Since I could not bring myself to part with any of it, I brought his things home with me and stacked the boxes in a corner of my room where they remain to this day. I wore one of his T-shirts to bed for a few nights because it held his scent, but it soon faded away and was replaced by my own. I hung it behind my bedroom door, never to be washed. I didn't want to risk any more of his things losing his essence, so I never wore anything else.

What I began doing at bedtime every night was holding one of his shirts to my face and breathing in deeply. It was like a piece of him went directly to my heart and as I stood there with my eyes closed, I was once again laying with my head on his chest. From there, I would pick up his black baseball cap and place the rim directly under my nose. In that instance, I was transported back to something I would do on the nights I visited him. As I was leaving, he would be sitting on the side of the bed. I'd stand in front of him, he'd lay his head against my chest, and I'd kiss the top of his head. Smelling his hat took me right back to those moments so I'd close my eyes and gently kiss the inside of his hat.

Next, I'd move on to his hair brush and sniff that, as well. I read somewhere that scent is the strongest sense tied to memory and I can honestly say that's true. I have continued doing this every night at bedtime since the day I brought his things home with me. If by chance I get into bed without completing my nightly ritual, I get right back up and do it. This is my way of kissing him goodnight and I'm so thankful for how long his scent has lasted.

After his apartment was empty, I had to call his landlord to return the key. Before doing so, I went back alone and walked slowly from room to room. I needed one last look, one last time in each room remembering what we'd said and done there. The sadness in my heart as I walked around was so deep and it was combined with a sense of disbelief that this was it. This was the last time I'd be in those rooms. Even though each room was empty, simply being there made me feel closer to Tyger. However, this was ending.

Handing over the key would mark another finale and I hated it. I stepped out onto the back porch and thought about how we would stand out there and see deer walking around in the woods behind the house, along the river bank. I noticed the one live plant that he owned was back there. His next door neighbor had moved out and left it behind, so he called me one day and said, "I think I'll keep this plant and see what I can do with it." He'd been watering it and it was doing well. I decided to bring it home with me and add it to my collection, so I put it in my car and waited for the landlord to arrive.

Once the key was returned and I started to drive away for the last time, I rode slowly past the house and was flooded with so many memories. After that day, I would sometimes ride out to the storage unit where his belongings were being kept. As strange as this may sound, I needed to visit his things to be near them. I would go and open the overhead door to the unit and immediately be greeted by his scent, the smell of his place, and his things. I would step inside and stand there looking around remembering where his possessions had once been and absorbing the familiar feeling they gave me. It was as though he was somehow still there because I could physically touch and see the things that had belonged to him and recall when he told me where he'd gotten this or that. It comforted me to be surrounded by what once had meant something to him.

I was thankful for the several videos and many photos I had of him. I enlarged some of the pictures and framed them, placing them in different rooms of my house. It helped to see him as he was; his smile reassured me. I was surprised by the comfort I received when I watched recordings of him. In the past, I'd wondered how anyone who'd suffered the loss of a loved one could ever watch the person on video. Wouldn't that intensify their longing and make them miss the person more? I found out it was exactly the opposite. Being able to hear Tyger speak and see him moving around made me feel like he was still here. I had a piece of him I could hold onto and experience someplace other than only in my mind.

There were times when I'd watch the videos and the tears would fall. That was part of missing him, but those images of the man I loved brought much more comfort than they did anguish. Having his things around me was a source of comfort and I needed so badly to feel him near.

I purchased a shadow box and put his New England Patriots jersey and hat inside and then hung them on a wall in my bedroom. I placed his slippers under a chair in my room where I could see them and remember how much he enjoyed wearing them. It may sound as if I was building a shrine to him and maybe I was. All I knew was it helped to see his things and to be able to reach out and touch them anytime I wanted. Anything that could bring the slightest relief from the constant aching in my heart was worth trying... and this helped.

I had so many memories of us and I held every one of them tightly in my heart. I would lay in bed and think back to the countless times we'd laid together. How he would always pull the blankets up and gently cover me with a tenderness that was almost indescribable. He would tuck me in and pull me close, my back up against him, feeling the warmth of his skin. As he held me tightly in his arms, I felt completely safe, totally protected, and wrapped in his love. Now, I lay in my bed, alone, thinking back to those beautiful moments and still able to close my eyes and remember exactly how it felt to touch him and to feel him touching me. In those moments, we were the only two people in the world and nothing else mattered.

How would I live the rest of my life without that ever happening again? How could I possibly go on without seeing that look of deep love in his eyes?

These were the questions I asked myself constantly. This couldn't be happening. He had to be right at home and all I had to do was call and he'd answer. There was no way he would just leave. He needed me as much as I needed him and it was impossible to believe everything we'd once shared had stopped. Never had I ever imagined there would be an end to us. How could something so beautiful and so perfect, have an ending?

When he held me tight in his arms, I'd snuggle in close and say, "This is my happy place."

I longed so badly to feel loved and protected again. I missed my happy place.

CHAPTER SEVEN
Alone in the Darkness

FOLLOWING THE LOSS OF A LOVED ONE, there comes a time when the phone calls and visits pretty much stop. It doesn't happen because people no longer care, they simply return to the normalcy of their lives. This was when I began assessing my situation and trying to figure out what to do with what was left of the world I now existed in.

For me, that was exactly what it was – existing. It certainly wasn't what I'd call living. I was drawing breath and my heart was beating, but those are merely bodily functions. My will to truly live or find beauty or enjoyment in anything had been replaced by deep sadness and missing the man I loved. Most of the time, I sat in painful disbelief over how much my life had changed. He was gone in an instant and the most difficult part was the silence. Having the communication between us stop was nearly impossible to adjust to.

To help fill this void, I continued with my Facebook posts and spoke out loud to him. No matter where I was, at home, in the car, at the cemetery, I told him whatever came to my mind as though he was standing right next to me. Writing to him was also helpful, so I kept a notebook on my nightstand and began penning letters to him at bedtime. Some nights it was difficult because the pages were so wet from my tears. I needed to pour my heart out in words, so that was what I did.

Where did I even begin to start picking up the pieces of what was once my life? I was absolutely consumed with sadness and so many memories of the man I loved more than life itself. The loneliness I felt wasn't a general feeling; I was longing for him and him only. There was nothing and no one who could fill that space.

How I missed his hairy chest. When he had spent those few days in the hospital months earlier, I remember the nurse coming in to remove the leads from a monitor he'd been wearing. She asked if he wanted to do it himself because she didn't want to hurt him if any hair was pulled out. He told her to go ahead and do it and as soon as she tugged off the first one, he said, "Ouch!" then laughed at her reaction. At discharge time, they sent an elderly lady with a wheelchair to escort him out. He insisted he didn't need it and could walk, but hospital policy stated he had to leave in a wheelchair.

So, he says to her, "You found a chair that'll fit me?"

She laughed and said, "Oh, yes, I did. This is the Cadillac of wheelchairs."

He and I both got a kick out of that because little did she know he drove a Cadillac.

She was the right match for him. Every remark he made, she came right back with a quick and funny answer. What a sight this little old lady pushing this great big guy in a wheelchair through the halls of the hospital.

These memories helped, but they also hurt at the same time. I was so grateful to be able to look back on them, yet so devastated that Tyger and I could never make new ones. I needed to find some way of consoling my broken heart.

I've always enjoyed reading, so I went to a local bookstore looking for anything that might help relieve this constant pain. I picked up a few books on grief and the grieving process, hoping, if nothing else, that I'd find out I wasn't completely losing my mind.

Since it was summer and the weather was nice, I'd go to the park and sit at a table under a tree with my books. Unfortunately, this task brought me little, if any, comfort. All the books seemed to be telling me about stages or how I should or should not be feeling. This did nothing to calm my spirit or help in any way. The words made me feel pushed toward something I wasn't ready for.

Not only that, but what I really wanted to know about was Tyger. Where had he gone? Was he all right? What was it like for him now? I'd always believed there was more to life than what we experience physically and in the existence of an afterlife. I'd never given much thought to what it might actually be like on the other side. My Christian upbringing taught me what the Bible said on the subject. Having lost both of my parents years earlier, death had touched my life before. I was sure they both had gone to heaven. This loss was entirely different, though, and I truly needed answers and more tangible proof that life continued beyond physical death.

On my next trip to the bookstore, I went in a different direction and selected books about the types of signs people had received from lost loved ones. These stories were so touching and the thought of being contacted by Tyger was quite exciting. As I read the author's words, I could feel the joy these communications had brought them. Some even offered tips on how to be more receptive to this new way of communicating. It was suggested that lying in bed in a relaxed state and extending your hand could lead to the sensation of your loved one holding it. They advised you to clear your mind, speak to your loved one, and ask them to touch your hand. It was disappointing when I tried this and felt no sensation at all.

Another suggestion was using meditation as a way of being more receptive to contact from the other side. That made sense, so I downloaded music to my iPod designed specifically to induce a meditative state. After multiple attempts, it just didn't seem to be working for me.

It wasn't long before I began asking myself, "What's wrong with me? Why don't I get any signs?" As I continued reading about the experiences others were having, it began to add to my sadness and make me feel even lonelier. I was almost jealous of what these other people were receiving. I couldn't understand what made them capable of receiving messages, yet I wasn't getting them. Tyger and I had been so connected in this life. That connection should've been strong enough to survive anything. Why wasn't he coming through? Was my grief somehow blocking messages he was trying to send?

I started to wonder if that was the problem, but I was so saddened by my disappointment it only made me fall deeper into grief and depression. It was a feeling of complete isolation.

Although I was raised Catholic, I had drifted away from religion and hadn't regularly attended church since I was a child. Once my mother quit telling me I *had* to go, I stopped going. I continued to believe in God, though, and at different stages in my adult life, I had studied the Bible. I considered myself a non-denominational Christian.

Since I'd found peace in the scriptures before, I decided to begin reading and searching for comfort in the word of God. I took a break from the bookstore and started bringing my Bible to the park and focusing on the New Testament. Reading the teachings of Jesus calmed my spirit. It also confirmed what I already believed to be true about the existence of another life beyond this physical world. I highlighted scriptures that spoke to my heart and would read them again at bedtime. The grief and sadness were still raw and real, but this offered moments of relief and I was so grateful.

Several times, it was said to me it was too bad I wasn't working because a job would provide a distraction from my grief. I disagreed with that. I was thankful for the time to be alone with my thoughts *without* any distractions. Financially I was stable thanks to the severance checks as well as collecting unemployment. There was no great urgency to find a job and add the stress of interviewing to my fragile state. I did, however, have obligations to fulfill as a recipient of unemployment. I was expected to attend workshops and be actively seeking opportunities.

Barely two weeks after Tyger passed way, I remember sitting through a workshop in a room full of people and feeling like an alien from another planet. Here I was listening to them talk about resumes and career choices when it was all I could do to brush my teeth and comb my hair every morning. As strange as this may sound, I also found it very surprising they didn't realize he was gone. It made no difference to me that not one person in the room had ever known Tyger, I felt like him leaving this world should have impacted these other people somehow. It almost angered me that it hadn't.

Outwardly, I must have appeared to be doing well. I'd begun eating again and I was showing up at these workshops, doing what was expected. My posts on social media were frequent and well-received by many. It seemed I was coping well. I was able to carry on conversations and even speak about Tyger without crying every time.

Often, I'd hear, "You're such a strong person Diane." To me, that sounded like the most ridiculous thing I'd ever heard. Strong? I was utterly dying inside, still hoping and praying God would call me home soon. I was terrified by the thought of making it to old age and struggling to find meaning in anything this ugly world had to offer since Tyger left. In no way did I consider myself to be strong.

My actions were driven by basic survival instinct. I kept moving because that was what had to be done; not because I wanted to. It was true that I was able to get through most days without constant tears, but I was still overwhelmed with sadness every night when I put my head on my pillow. No matter where I was or what I did, I was constantly aware of what was missing.

Regardless of how strong I may have appeared to others, what I really wanted to do was lock myself in a closet and never come out. Time kept right on moving, though, whether I liked it or not. Time ticked forward and I spent every minute missing my man. I did not like being here without him, not one bit.

There were times I would question whether or not I was losing my mind. I'd go a day or two where I'd feel almost like I could cope and then, the familiar pain would come back stronger than before. Tyger's brother was storing the Cadillac in his yard and I had to stop by his house one day. I knew the car was there, but I wasn't prepared for how I'd feel when I saw it. Sophia was with me and it had been snowing. She went over to the car and started to brush the snow off.

She said, "Nani, I'm cleaning Mike's car, but I'm being careful so I don't scratch it."

As I stood there watching her, I was touched by how gentle she was and her awareness of what that car had meant to him. She cleared as much of it as she could, then started playing in the small drifts on the side of the driveway. After a few minutes, she began drawing hearts in the snow. Big hearts, little ones... she had hearts of all sizes on the ground surrounding the Caddy. Suddenly, I was flooded with memories of Tyger and me riding in the car together. That car *was* him. He'd put so much into it to make it unique and his own. I felt a lump swelling in my throat and a wave of sadness washed over me.

We weren't there very long, but simply seeing his car took me to a place I hadn't expected to go. I cried silent tears the whole ride home, completely heartbroken at the thought of Tyger never driving that car again. Overcome with memories of going out for ice cream or to our favorite seafood places in the summer... the time he put a movie in the DVD player and I watched *The Green Hornet* as he drove... the day we went to the park so he could take pictures of me next to the Caddy (he said he needed a picture of his two prized possessions)... the custom hood ornament of a flying lady he named Diane... how he'd pull up in front of my house to pick me up and I'd hear the bass thumping before he could even send the text to let me know he'd arrived. It was always just one word, "Here," and I'd hurry outside, slide into the front seat and we'd kiss.

So many wonderful memories.

Sophia was so sweet. When we got home, she saw I was upset and then she drew a picture of Tyger and me dancing together to cheer me up. After seeing his car, it took two days before I could function again. I spent that time on the couch and didn't even bother to shower. I was immersed in sadness and consumed by a deep longing for the way things once were.

There were so many unwelcome changes in my life.

My cell phone—which had once been a source of joy whenever I got a call or text from him—now became a constant reminder that he was gone. Before he passed, I would carry the phone with me from room to room, never wanting to miss a message or call from my love. Now, everything was different and I no longer needed the device with me constantly. If someone did try to reach me, I could get back to them whenever I had time. It didn't matter if I missed a call or text anymore.

I was so incredibly thankful for the texts from Tyger that were saved on my phone. I would read our old conversations constantly. It was comforting to read his words because I could hear his voice in the way he wrote.

The most painful part was reading the last few words we sent to each other on his last night. The last two words he ever sent to me were simply, "okay, cool." And, just like that, it was over. There would be no new messages, so those last two words became frozen in time for me.

I will keep his messages forever and I will never get tired of reading them over and over again. The same was true for his cell number notated in my phone as "My Man." Even though that number is no longer active, it has to remain as was, never to be removed from my contacts. Not ever.

I'd be driving through the town where we'd both grown up. I'd look at the streets and sidewalks remembering stories he'd told me about going here or there. How could it be that he would never walk or drive on these streets again? It made no sense to me that they were still there, but he was not. If I happened to be out in the early evening, it was unbelievable that I couldn't drive to his place and find him laying across his bed. The house was still there, so shouldn't he be there too? Waiting for me to arrive?

More than once, my heartache took control and I cried my eyes out as I drove on the roads we'd once traveled together. There were times when I would scream and pound on the steering wheel – sad, angry, hurt, lonely, and completely heartbroken. I would ride around until I pulled myself together. If my boys were home when I got back, I didn't want them to see me in this state. After all, I was their mother and the one who usually made things better. Even though they knew I was grieving and struggling through my sadness, I tried to avoid having breakdowns in front of them.

When I arrived home after these episodes, I would take my time going up the four steps to the porch wondering exactly what there was to do once I entered the house. I couldn't call Tyger and he wouldn't be stopping by. He wouldn't be calling to let me know he was in so I could head over there to see him. What exactly was the point of anything? I had nothing to look forward to since he'd left. No excitement or anticipation of upcoming plans. Just nothing and more nothing.

The only thing I could count on was the constant ache in my chest. A heavy feeling which was a mixture of sadness, fear, and a fair amount of disbelief that any of this could be real. It was the complete opposite of how I'd felt the entire time he and I were together. I supposed I was grieving for the loss of our happiness, as well as the beautiful feeling I woke up with every morning and fell asleep with every night. All of that had left with him and I missed it so much.

How I missed Tyger's laugh. It was the most wonderful, deep, belly laugh. There was a silliness about him I absolutely loved. Whenever I'd ask a question he didn't want to answer, he'd say, "Huh? What?" acting as though he had no idea what I was saying. I longed for the times I'd just listen to him talk. Whether he was telling about his past or sharing his vision for his future jazz club, he had a descriptive way of speaking that put you right there, in the story. Never did I ever imagine a day would come when it would all stop. Yet, here I was in a living nightmare I couldn't wake up from. I was longing for that familiar feeling of being deeply loved and trying to come to terms with the harsh reality of life without him.

Having to go on with the knowledge that I still existed in this world and Tyger did not made me feel completely alone. I felt isolated, insignificant and very small. Picture a scene from a movie when they show a wide shot of a big city, people hustling and bustling everywhere and then the camera zooms in on one, small detail in the middle of all that movement. That was me. I was a tiny speck watching all this activity taking place around me and unable to figure out where I belonged. I had no clue whatsoever where I fit in.

Everything moved for me in slow motion while others carried on as though nothing had happened. It didn't matter how many phone calls I got from family and friends or how many people stopped by to see me, without Tyger, the aloneness never went away. The shock of him disappearing from my life so suddenly altered my perception of every single thing. If I heard about a movie release, my first thought was how sad it was he would never get to see it. When Sophia would say something funny or learn something new, I'd think of what his reaction would be and how he loved hearing about what she said and did. Wrapped up in the many things I was grieving for was the disappointment of the fresh experiences he was missing out on.

Heartache, tears, and the rare but occasional smile a memory would bring, pretty much summed up my existence. The disappointment of not receiving signs from him from the other side merely intensified my grief. Since his passing, I hadn't even dreamt of him, not even once. He was on my mind constantly, but I'd wake up full of sadness because once again he hadn't appeared in my dreams.

Where was he?

Why can't I feel him near?

Always more questions, but never any answers. I began to feel attached to the isolation, comfortable in my heartache. I held onto it tight and made it my connection to him. Rather than continue looking for signs that didn't seem to be coming, I decided to accept that I was alone living on my private island of grief. It was a dark place for sure; however, it left no room for disappointment so my heart felt it was safe to stay there.

This had become my new normal.

CHAPTER EIGHT
Searching for Answers

HOW COULD SUCH PURE HAPPINESS just be taken away?

I was struggling with the issue and couldn't make sense of it. Why did this happen? Was I being punished for something I'd done in the past? These were the questions going through my mind.

"Everything happens for a reason."

Those words were said to me so many times, but what could that reason possibly be? I decided to try the bookstore again in the hopes of finding something to help me. Somehow, I ended up in the section where books on near-death experiences were kept. I picked a couple and went home to see if this topic could help me make sense of things.

The first book I read on the subject was *90 Minutes in Heaven* by Don Piper. The story is his account of dying, visiting heaven, then returning to his body ninety minutes later. As I learned about his experience, I was surprised by how much comfort it brought me. His description of this beautiful place of pure love began to ease my worries of whether or not Tyger was all right. I went back and bought several more books by different people who'd had near-death experiences. I was completely intrigued by what I was learning.

As I finished book after book, I noticed the differences in each individual experience. What was even more striking, though, were the similarities. There was always this feeling of being completely loved and accepted with a total lack of judgment or condemnation. Each experience had a connection to a higher power, a source who seemed to be pure love and light.

Delving deeper and deeper into what these people had witnessed, I began to slowly emerge from the pitch blackness of what my world had become. It seemed no matter how much I learned about this subject, I needed to know more.

It was also around this time that I began going to church. As I've said before, I've always believed in God. I longed to become more in tune with my spiritual self, so I went there seeking a spiritual connection. It also gave me an opportunity to focus on something beyond the agony of grief and find relief for my heartache. There were so many voices speaking love and God's word. Being a part of that made me feel connected to the source of all that is.

Each week, I was there to praise, sing, and worship and to simply give thanks for being alive. Surrendering the burden of pain into God's hands was what sparked my desire to give life another chance. It directed me toward the path to healing. At my lowest points and my darkest moments, it was God's love which carried me when I didn't have the strength to do so myself. I began to realize God wasn't finished with me yet and, as badly as I'd wanted my life to end, I didn't get to decide that. There was a purpose for my being here which went beyond what I could see in the present moment, so I had to trust His wisdom and His plan.

As I became completely enveloped in the church atmosphere, I began to see something beyond my grief, to catch a glimpse of hope. Being a part of a loving environment was exactly what my soul needed. That experience along with what I was discovering about the afterlife expanded my belief that there was much more to life than this physical existence.

I was beginning to have moments of peace and my thirst for knowledge of the afterlife continued to grow. What stood out to me was the people who were writing these accounts came from all walks of life; some very religious, some not at all. Yet, their experiences still held the same message: *we are here to learn and to love.*

One night, I was reading a book written by a female doctor who'd had a near-death experience and then, years later, she lost her nineteen-year-old son. She was questioning why he had been taken. The answer she received was that although his time here had been short, his work in this life was done.

All at once it became so clear to me. It was almost as if I could hear God speaking to my heart and telling me it was not about me. It was *never* about me.

It was about Tyger. His work in this life was done, so he made his transition into the next.

In the moments that followed, I laid there staring up at the ceiling with tears rolling down my cheeks, saying to God, "I get it now. I get it. I understand why. I need you to know, God, I don't like the fact that he had to go, but it's clear to me now."

Alone in my room at 2:00 a.m., so much was revealed to me. The reason God had set us on a path to find each other suddenly made perfect sense. Tyger and I spoke so many times about how people probably couldn't figure out how he and I ended up together, especially those who knew him during his troubled past. There couldn't possibly be a more unlikely couple. Yet, there we were so happy and in love, experiencing a level of joy neither of us had ever known before. God wanted the two of us to develop a deep, true love. That was exactly how our story unfolded, slowly and naturally over time. Before we knew it, we were very much in love. A love so real it could transcend anything including the illusion of separation death brings.

It also made sense to me why God had chosen that day for Tyger to make his transition. It was a day filled with happiness when he really enjoyed himself and knew he was loved. This revelation was such an emotional awakening for me, but I was so grateful for it.

As wonderful as it was to be given this understanding, it certainly wasn't a miraculous cure for my grief. I felt completely broken and my heart hurt constantly. The ache in my chest as I cried out for him was an actual, physical sensation. I would pray for relief from the agony and be blessed with periods of no tears.

Almost immediately following this relief, I'd become overwhelmed with guilt. *Where are the tears? Why don't I feel? Where is the grief I'd prayed for relief from?*

Suddenly, it would return and wash over me like a giant wave of despair. There were times when I'd be going about my day and realize Tyger wasn't here anymore. He wouldn't be calling or texting me, I wouldn't pass him on the road, cook him a meal, or tell him about something funny that had happened. Those moments were like a knife to my heart; the deepest, most devastating sadness, as well as the loneliest feeling I'd ever known. A hurt so intense I would drop to my knees and then pray for help. My life had become a non-stop roller coaster of emotion and all I could do was hold on for the ride.

This was a completely unfamiliar experience for me despite the fact that I'd survived the loss of both parents. My mother passed away very unexpectedly eighteen years earlier. My dad succumbed to cancer nine years after that. I'd managed to find my way through and I wondered how I'd been able to do that. I remembered how much it hurt to lose them, yet I didn't recall feeling this level of hopelessness. I'd loved them both dearly and to this day, miss them terribly. How had I found the strength to go on? The only explanation I could come up with was somewhere in our genetic makeup, we expect to lose our parents during our lifetime. We certainly never want to lose them and the heartache is very real. Somehow, this seems to be the natural order of things.

(I certainly don't mean to imply my sorrow is greater than that of someone who has lost a parent. I'm describing my personal experience.)

All I knew was this loss had been different. This was not supposed to happen and even with the answers I'd been given, I could not understand why our happiness had to end. This simply wasn't anything I'd ever considered... an ending to what we shared.

When you meet someone who is everything you've ever wanted, everything you'd never even known you *needed,* the expectation is it will continue forever. There was never any talk of "when this is over." It was always, "What will we experience tomorrow?" So, to lose that person and to suddenly have them disappear from your life, the heart and mind cannot make sense of it. I had never expected him to go and I believed right up until the last second, neither had he. He fought to stay and I fought to keep him here. In the end, though, it wasn't up to either of us.

As much as I hated to admit it, leaving the physical world when he did was part of his journey. Coming to that realization certainly didn't ease my suffering in any way, but I knew I would have to come to terms with that and someday learn to accept it.

My posts on Facebook continued to be a way to express what I was experiencing at the moment. I had begun making observations about the changes going on within me. One noticeable difference was my inability to wish anyone a happy birthday for a period of time following Tyger's death. I would receive notifications almost every day telling me it was the birthday of a friend, but I couldn't bring myself to wish anyone a happy anything. To me, it felt like I'd be lying, so I chose to say nothing. After a while, I was able to at least write, "Enjoy your day" or something to that effect, but I still couldn't use the word "happy." It took a couple of months before I was able to wish someone a happy birthday and feel like it was genuine.

Another observation was my complete lack of desire to listen to any sort of music in the car after Tyger died. The CDs in the stereo were out of the question. They would only remind me of the many times I'd driven to his house listening to those songs. The same was true for the radio, so I chose silence instead. As time went on, I was able to listen to music again and I knew my ability to re-introduce these things into my life were signs I was moving forward.

The responses I would get to my social media posts were totally unexpected. People complimented my ability to express myself. I was often told to keep posting because I was helping others without even realizing it. In all honesty, I was posting for purely selfish reasons because it was helping me. I hadn't considered how my words would affect anyone else, yet I was told numerous times I was giving a voice to those who were suffering and couldn't find the right words to express themselves. So, I continued to write... for myself as well as anyone else who could relate.

Although my state of mind was in turmoil, the majority of the time there were things that remained constant. The first was the gratefulness in my heart for God having brought Tyger and me together. Each night, I began my prayers by thanking God for guiding us to find one another and allowing us to experience such an amazing love (I still do this.) I realize sometimes after losing a loved one, people blame God for taking them away, but that wasn't how I viewed what happened. Instead, my focus was on how much my life improved from the moment Tyger and I connected and how we lifted each other up so high.

Early in my grief, a friend said to me, "Diane, don't let this change you. Stay the person you are." I guess it would've been easy to become a miserable person, angry at the world for what was taken from me. That wasn't the path I chose, though. Instead, I focused on how blessed I was to have experienced such happiness and love. It was impossible for me to be the exact person I was before because grief completely shifts and rearranges things at the deepest level. I recognized, however, that the greatest way to honor the man I loved was to continue being the woman he fell in love with.

The other thing that remained constant was a complete absence of any feelings of regret. Tyger and I never took each other for granted. We expressed our love for one another constantly through words and actions. There was no sense of things left unsaid because we shared our feelings and held nothing back. So, yes, I felt sadness from missing him, but regret? Absolutely not. We had set out from the beginning to "get it all in" and we had succeeded in doing that.

Of course, I would've loved to have had more time with him, but in all honesty, one hundred years still wouldn't have been enough. To some, our three years may not appear to be very long, but we managed to share a plenitude of love together, more than some people experience in a lifetime. It's not about the number of anniversaries you accumulate, it's what's done during your time together that matters most. There are many who search their whole lives to discover what we'd found in one another.

Our lives were so intertwined and I could see his influence in every room of my home. One night, I collapsed on my bedroom floor in tears. I was home alone, so I poured out all the sadness I was feeling at that moment. As I began to lift myself up, I swept my hand across the rug and remembered the day Tyger took me to the store to buy it. After I moved in, I'd mentioned there were hardwood floors in my bedroom and how I wanted to get an area rug to cover part of it. We went and picked one out together.

When I stood up, my eyes caught the group of pictures he had given to me on the wall. He'd seen them somewhere and thought the shades of blue would look nice in my room. He'd been right. Above my bed was a small shelf I'd gotten from him. He had two of them, so I helped him hang one above his bed and he gave the other one to me. When he came to see how I'd set mine up, he decided it looked better than his. He said, "Wow, it looks very nice. You did a great job," all the while, playfully hugging my neck in the crook of his arm, pretending to have me in a headlock before leaning down to kiss me.

The stereo system Tyger had given me was set up in my living room. When he found out I listened to music on my computer, he told me he'd give me his stereo since it was sitting around collecting dust. We laughed when he brought it here because it really was dusty. After that, he would say the stereo was "looking at him funny" every time he stopped by because it was so well taken care of and dust-free at my place.

In the kitchen was the Keurig, his Christmas gift to me a few years back and the new microwave he'd bought me after my old one finally died. In the bathroom were the candle holders he'd brought by after I'd redecorated. His style was the inspiration behind the way I'd set up so many things. Even though it was painful missing him so much, seeing and feeling his influence comforted me, as well. I was surrounded by so many beautiful reminders.

As I continued making my way through this maze of grief, I began to focus more on the meaning of things. I'd learned much about what it was like in the afterlife, and at least, had some understanding that his death wasn't a punishment directed towards me. I wanted to know more and my continued research into the world of near-death experiences was opening my mind to so many wonderful possibilities.

I began wondering if maybe he had tried reaching out.

Maybe we were still connected.

Maybe, just maybe...

CHAPTER NINE
Am I Imagining Things?

AS DESPERATE AS I WAS to receive a sign or a message from my love, I was hesitant to really believe the little things happening around me were from him. My initial reaction was usually to question, "Could that have been him?"

Having had absolutely no experience receiving afterlife communications, I was extremely cautious. I wanted to hear from Tyger so badly, but I was afraid to read things into something that simply wasn't there. Having said that, I was still open to the possibility and when I spoke to him, I constantly asked for a sign. I needed to know he was here in some way, watching over me. My heart was certain love never died, but I wanted something I could hold on to. A sign or a message to let me know he would never leave and he'd always be nearby, loving me from the other side.

One of the first things to catch my attention as a possible sign happened the day his brothers came to visit. As they were leaving, they invited me to their sister's house. The family was getting together and I was more than welcome to join them.

Tyger and I had visited her together a few times. She is the oldest sibling and such a gentle, kind, loving soul. Since their mother passed away years earlier, she inherited the role of matriarch. Tyger loved his family very much but always had a special place in his heart for his oldest sister. She had always made me feel so welcome and I hadn't seen her since his passing. I decided to go for a little while to see how she was doing. It took me around twenty minutes to get ready after they left before getting in the car to head over.

Since I had been to her house more than once, I wasn't concerned about how to get there. As I got closer, I started thinking about the streets and trying to recall where Tyger had turned. I wasn't so sure I knew the way. As these thoughts were going through my mind, I noticed a vehicle up ahead turn off of a side street onto the road I was on. Instantly, I recognized it was his brother's car. They had made a stop after leaving my house and somehow ended up directly in front of me. I followed them right to her front door.

Did Tyger cause that? I wondered...

We sat and talked, reminiscing about memories we each had of him and expressing our disbelief that he was gone. I was sitting at the dining room table facing the sliding glass doors leading out to the deck. There was a flower box hanging on the outside rail and as I admired the blooms, a hummingbird appeared and hovered above them. The bird seemed to be looking in my direction and I thought how small, but beautiful it was.

All of a sudden, a memory came back to me from a few months earlier. Tyger was having an oil change on his SUV and had gone outside to wait for his vehicle. As he sat there, a hummingbird flew over to some nearby flowers and he called to tell me about it.

"Have you ever seen a hummingbird?" he asked.

I answered, "Not too often, but I have seen them."

He said, "Well, I'm sitting at this table outside the Quick Lube place and there's one right next to me. It's not much bigger than a bug."

That was about the extent of the call; he simply wanted to tell me about his impression of the hummingbird. It didn't seem at all unusual that he would call to tell me about this because we always shared everything with each other. Now, here was this hummingbird, directly across from me, at eye level, hovering above his sister's flowers.

Could it be him?

Having lived alone for so many years, my guy ate quite a bit of take-out food. He had his favorite spots like a pizza place or the shops that made the best grinders, as they're called in New England. For anyone who doesn't know what a grinder is, you may know it as a hoagie or Subway sandwich. There's a shop in town, D'Elia's, that's been around forever. One day, I mentioned to him I hadn't been there since I was in high school.

His response to that was, "What? You've got to be kidding me. We'll have to get lunch there one of these days."

Not too long after that conversation, he asked me to meet him there to grab a couple of grinders. I couldn't make it so we decided we'd do it some other time but we never got the chance to go. The weekend after he passed, my cousin stopped by carrying a brown paper bag.

She said, "I didn't know what to bring so I stopped at D'Elia's and got you a couple of grinders."

I burst into tears, telling her how Tyger and I had planned to go there, but hadn't gotten a chance to. She felt bad about making me cry and said she was planning to stop at a different shop but at the last minute decided to stop there.

A few minutes later my phone rang. It was Angy telling me she was on her way over. She asked, "Did you eat? Do you want a grinder from D'Elia's?" I was still being very cautious, but started wondering what to make of this.

Was it him?

During the procession from the church to the cemetery, we noticed the car carrying Tyger to his place of rest was a Cadillac. That impressed us because of Tyger having owned a Cadillac. Although his was an older model Cadillac DeVille, no one would have ever guessed how old it was after what he'd added to it. His car was an eye catcher for sure. We followed behind the hearse in his Cadillac. His nephew was the driver and Tyger's son and best friend rode with us. We marveled at how Tyger's last ride ever was in a Cadillac and how much he would've liked that.

A couple of weeks later, I was talking to the funeral director who handled Tyger's service. He asked if I had a few minutes because he wanted to share something with me. He explained it's common practice for funeral homes to loan their cars out to one another when needed. The day of Tyger's service it just so happened that all of the funeral home's cars—three Lincolns—were being used. The director called a fellow funeral director, explained his situation, and asked if he had a car available he could use for the day. His friend proceeded to tell him yes, it was brand new—purchased the day before—and it hadn't been used yet. The only thing was it was a Cadillac and not a Lincoln, so he hoped that wouldn't be a problem. Knowing Tyger had driven a Cadillac, he said he had a hard time believing what he was hearing. As for me, I was sure, by this point in his story, my jaw must've been hanging open. He went on to say how rare it was that all of his cars would be unavailable on the same day and it almost never happened.

There was a voice in my head asking the questions my heart was afraid to hope for. This couldn't possibly be a long string of coincidences. It must be him, right? Is he making these things happen to let us know he's still here? Oh, how I wanted that to be the case. I *needed* it to be him. The weight of my grief was causing doubt. I wanted signs but was afraid to really recognize them out of fear of feeling more pain. They were certainly making me pay attention, though, and, at least, I'd begun asking questions.

One morning, as I was waking up—kind of caught between sleep and being awake—I began to hear loud music. It wasn't a song I recognized. To this day, it's not a song I've ever heard. The rhythm was a reggae style and a male voice kept repeating the same words, *"It's the good life, it's the city, it's the easy way I live."* As I became more alert, I was annoyed that this music had woken me up. *Who is playing music that loud before eight in the morning?*

I opened my eyes and slowly realized I was hearing this song in my head. The sound wasn't coming through my ears at all; it was actually inside of me. I'd never experienced anything like this and had no idea what to make of it. Where had this song come from? To this very day, I can still remember the melody exactly as I heard it back then.

Oh, my goodness. Was this Tyger's way of telling me he was living and it was good?

At that very moment, I began to sit up and take notice. This was *not* something I'd imagined; my eyes were wide open, I was aware of my surroundings and knew without a doubt I was not hearing this music with my ears. It began slowly fading away as I became more fully awake, but it was definitely real. Wait... hadn't I read in one of my many books that it's easiest for communications to come through in twilight moments, between sleep and awake?

I think it's really him. He's alive on the other side and he's trying to convince me I am not imagining things.

What an amazing revelation that was. He's not really gone. I haven't lost him. He's still here with me. My heart leaped with joy over such a wonderful feeling. These events had been happening all along, but once I began to acknowledge what was going on, I was able to see those earlier occurrences through new eyes. That was the reason I'd suddenly wanted to look through his old phones. He'd pushed me to do that because he knew he'd saved those messages and it would be an amazing gift of love. He was also the one who set things in motion to have his brothers end up in front of me on my way to his sister's house. He sent the hummingbird so I'd remember his phone call to me months before. No wonder my cousins were drawn to that one grinder shop even though there were plenty of others in town. Neither one of them knew about the lunch date my love and I were supposed to have, but Tyger knew and he knew I'd remember. As for the situation with the car at his funeral, there was absolutely, positively no way his last ride was going to be in a Lincoln. That entire scenario was orchestrated by him in order for his physical remains to have their final ride in a Caddy, which was the vehicle make he loved.

We had decided to go forward with the event Tyger had been organizing with his nephew and best friend. It was held about a month after he passed and done as a tribute to him. I drove his SUV (a Saturn Outlook) that day and we used it to move the sound equipment to the marina where the event was held. When I arrived at his friend's house, I put the Saturn in park and turned the engine off. As I stepped out, I noticed it was still running so I got back in to make sure the ignition was in the "off" position. It was, so I thought maybe once I shut the door, the engine would stop. However, when I did that the engine continued running.

We loaded the equipment and drove to the marina. When we arrived, I parked, turned the ignition off, and removed the key. The engine was still running. Several people tried to get it to stop, but it wouldn't. Key in or out, it didn't matter. We could not get the engine to turn off. Finally, we left it running while we got the equipment set up and everything organized.

When Tyger's nephew arrived, I explained what was going on. He tried to get it to turn off. Finally, he was about to disconnect the battery when he decided to try the key one more time. Miraculously, it worked. After running for several hours, the engine finally stopped. Was this Tyger's way of letting us know he was right there overseeing everything we did? It made perfect sense to me because he was always involved in every detail of any event. I believed he needed his presence to be felt.

Later that afternoon, I drove the Saturn again and stopped at the cemetery to speak with him. I turned the key and it shut off with no problem.

"I'm here, baby, and I'm driving the Saturn. See it there? Feels good to be in your vehicle. I feel so close to you. I know that was you keeping it running today. You were making sure we did things right. Thank you for that. I love you."

I made a few more stops and the SUV shut off and started back up every time just fine.

As I replayed these events in my mind, it was so obvious to me that it was Tyger. How had I not recognized it before? I was so excited to know he could communicate with me and when I spoke to him, he could hear me. All the wonderful experiences I had only read about were happening and available to me.

It definitely required patience and some learning on my part, but the most important lesson was to stop doubting. If something happened that I thought was a sign, it probably was. My heart had known this all along, but could it have been my mind causing the problem? Maybe it was a form of self-protection that had been in place until I was ready for this knowledge; this amazing world opening up to me.

The best analogy I could think of to describe this form of communication was to compare it to using a set of walkie-talkies. In order for them to work, both radios have to be on. If the person on the receiving end has their unit off, then the other person can talk all day and no one will hear a word of it. Once the receiver turns their switch *on*, they are able to hear what's being said and the lines of communication are then open.

I began dreaming about him. Sometimes these dreams were difficult to interpret, but they all had one important detail in common. In every single one, he had died, but was somehow able to come back and we were aware of it. We would talk about things that happened at his funeral or since then. As the dream continued, it never seemed strange to us in any way that he had died and returned.

In the first dream, I distinctly remember being terrified to let him out of my sight because I was so afraid I'd never see him again. I studied every detail of his face, trying to memorize everything, telling him how hard it had been since he'd left and how much I missed him. In another dream, he told me about a new blanket he had bought because we had taken all his blankets when we packed his things after he died. There were other dreams where I remember wanting so badly to call him, but knowing deep down that I couldn't or trying to do so with him never answering. The one time he did answer, we spoke for a few seconds and then his voice got softer and softer until I couldn't hear him anymore. Another dream was of him in the hospital lying in a queen sized bed with a pillow top mattress. We were sitting on the bed talking and he told me how his brother had insisted the hospital find him a comfortable bed after all he'd been through with dying and coming back.

Discovering he was able to send signs and messages was so amazing, but left me wanting more. In need of something more tangible, I began to consider seeing a medium. Of course, I'd never thought about doing this before and with so many different avenues to choose from, I had no idea what to do. This was another one of those things I couldn't discuss with anyone because people had already offered their ideas on the subject. "Don't go to a medium. That's the devil talking." I wasn't interested in anyone else's opinion, the majority of them had never experienced the heartache that had now become my life. I believed strongly that death was nothing more than a transition and our loved ones had the ability to communicate. I simply needed to find someone to make a direct connection between Tyger and me.

For a while, I'd been hearing about a medium, Matt Fraser, who was becoming quite well known in New England. I watched several videos of his and segments he'd done on local TV shows. When I checked his schedule, I found out he was holding an event at the casino I formerly worked for. After lots of thought and going back and forth, I decided to buy a ticket and go. It was a risk attending a large gathering like this and there was no guarantee I'd get a reading. It was open seating and Matt went around the room selecting random tables or rows of seats and speaking for whoever comes through for that particular group of people.

I was sure Tyger would come through, why wouldn't he?

I spent the entire week before asking him to please be there and I even gave him a code word to say. I chose "monsters" because that's how Tyger referred to an upper part of my anatomy that he particularly enjoyed. "Have him say monsters, baby. Then I'll know it's really you," I said to Tyger in the days leading up to the reading. When I arrived in the ballroom, I chose a seat at the end of a row. It seemed more likely that I'd get a reading that way. As the room filled up, I started to get concerned I wouldn't be selected. I stayed hopeful though and focused all thoughts on my love, trying to relay through my mind how badly I needed to hear from him.

It was incredible being there and hearing the beautiful communications to people from their loved ones on the other side. The reactions of those receiving the messages were so touching. Tears of joy for some and even some laughter for others. I found myself crying and laughing right along with them because I understood their need to hear something... anything. It was obvious those who'd crossed over still maintained their personalities and sense of humor. I'd learned that in the many books I'd read and it definitely came across in the readings.

As Matt made his way around the room, I wanted so desperately for him to call my row. He approached the side I was sitting on and began walking directly toward me. I was near the back of the room and as he got closer I was so excited, I was going to hear something direct. I actually began feeling light-headed and I couldn't believe this was really happening.

He stopped right next to me and asked the row behind mine to stand up. Then, he began doing readings for them. After that row, he moved to another section of the room and following a few more readings, the event was over.

My anticipation was instantly replaced with disappointment.

When I got up from my seat and began making my way toward the door, I felt like I had weights attached to my body. Not only was my heart heavy in my chest, my entire being seemed weighed down with sadness.

Once again, I was filled with despair and all I wanted to do was run out of there and get to my car so I could cry. The room was so crowded it took forever for the lines to move so I had to control my emotions as we slowly made our way toward the door. At last, I was out into the casino and I raced to the parking garage as fast as I could. The tears fell as I got closer to my car. By the time I got in, I had broken into sobs.

Why did this happen? Why didn't I get a reading? Hadn't he seen my love standing next to me, wanting to speak?

I continued to ask these questions as I drove, trying hard to focus on the road through my tears. After several minutes, the tears slowed down and I started to remember I hadn't eaten anything before the event. There was no way I was going home to cook, so I decided to stop at Burger King. This was an odd choice for me because I hadn't been to a fast food restaurant in a while. That was the place that came to mind, so I stopped and went inside.

Standing in line reading the menu, I thought about getting a Whopper Jr. with some fries and a drink. A thought came almost immediately:

Get a Whopper with cheese.

My response to that thought was: *No, a Whopper Jr. is good enough, I don't need a whole whopper.*

Instantly, the next thought was: *You want a Whopper with cheese.*

By then, the young man behind the counter asked for my order. To my surprise, I ordered a Whopper with cheese with fries and a soda.

When he handed me my food, I found a table, sat down, and ate every single bite of the sandwich and every last French fry. Afterward, I felt so much better. I went home, put my pajamas on, and relaxed for the night. I realized the visit to Burger King was Tyger's idea along with my unexpected order. My spirit was listening and he confirmed he had been with me all along.

I made the decision that night to never again try a group reading. Someday, when I was ready, I would go for a private reading where it was one on one.

Lesson learned.

I continued absorbing anything I could get my hands on about the afterlife and those who had experienced what lies beyond this physical existence. I purchased no less than ten books on the subject and became a regular customer at a local bookstore.

One story that spoke directly to my heart was Lyn Ragan's *Wake Me Up! Love and the Afterlife.* As I read about her heartbreaking experience of losing the love of her life in an unexpected tragedy, it was as if she was telling my story. I could feel the pain in her words as well as the anguish she was living in. It was so close to what I was experiencing I had to reach out to her on Facebook to share what I was going through and how I was able to relate to her feelings.

I was surprised when she replied to my comment. Reading about her experiences validated the messages I was receiving from Tyger and it let me know I wasn't the only person on Earth who was torn between gratitude for the gifts he was sending and the sadness of missing him terribly.

My thirst for knowledge became a bit expensive, though, so I decided to get a library card and begin checking out books on the subject. That was a wonderful decision and looking back, I have to wonder if it had been my idea at all or if Tyger had whispered to my soul and I had responded by doing it.

Sophia spoke of Mike so often. I wondered if he was communicating with her directly or at least through her. She would mention things about him casually and drew pictures of him or all of us together. Although the two of them were extremely close in this life, the amount of time she spent speaking of him made me think he had to be contacting her in some way. She would mention, out of the blue, that she'd spoken with Mike on the bus on her way home from school.

There was a day Sophia, Aaron, and I were watching a football game on TV. We told her Mikey liked the Patriots, so we were watching the game for him.

She immediately answered that Mike was watching, too, he was sitting, "right there" and she pointed to an empty chair.

My son and I looked at each other as if to say, "Does she really see him?"

I didn't want to scare her or make her think there was something wrong with her seeing him, so I said, "Oh, that's good. I'm glad he's watching."

On Sunday mornings, when she and I would sit down for breakfast, she would point out which chair Mike was sitting in so I wouldn't accidentally plop down on him.

This child, who had just turned six-years-old, spent so much of her time speaking of him. She actually said to me one day, "Mike told me to tell you he loves you because you're so beautiful."

This brought tears to my eyes, but I was always careful about my reactions because I didn't want her to feel she was upsetting me in any way. Oftentimes, when I was feeling really sad, she would go in my room, get his baseball cap, and then hand it to me so I could smell it. When I gave it back, she would do the same. His hat held special meaning for her because whenever he'd come over the first thing he'd do was pick her up. She'd snatch his cap off and throw it right on the floor. I wasn't sure why she did it, but it became their "thing" and she did it every time. Now, here she was sniffing it because it reminded her of him.

I said to her, "Soph, Mike's hat smells like his head."

Her answer every time was, "No, it smells like his body."

No matter how many times I tried to convince her otherwise, she wouldn't budge... it smelled like his body and that was it.

It amazed me that she was so young, yet he never seemed to be far from her thoughts.

One day, we were riding in the car and she asked, "Nani, if we hit another reindeer who's going to rescue us?"

I explained that we would call the police and they would come and help.

It was clear to me that Mike had made her feel safe and she knew he would protect us. She actually told me she loved Mike because he made her feel, "not scared of anything."

Something else she told me was she loved Mike, but felt bad that she'd been too shy to tell him when he was alive.

"It's all right," I told her. "Mike knew she loved him very much."

As we were riding to the beach one day, she said, "It's okay that I never told Mike I love him because he has all the proof he needs."

I said, "That's right, honey. He knows how much you love him."

She said, "No, it's because I always wanted to be around him. That's all the proof he needs."

Once again, this was a six-year-old child saying this. At such a young age, she had already figured out loving someone wasn't about material things or spending money. It was in the time you were willing to share with them that said it all. She was aware that her excitement, when they were together, was enough for him to know she loved him. It didn't matter she'd never told him directly. As the expression goes, "Out of the mouths of babes." What an incredible moment it was when she shared her thoughts with me.

The knowledge that Tyger was still with us was so comforting and brought moments of pure joy. At the same time, I was painfully aware that his physical presence was missing. My heart became a place where grief and joy coexisted and every so often, one would overpower the other. Being loved by this incredible soul had brought happiness to my life I'd never known. That feeling was still a part of me. It lived in all the beautiful memories we'd made together. On the other side of that was the pain of missing him physically. I longed to feel his touch, wishing we could make new memories. In this conflicted state, I realized grief was something that defies explanation. I would have moments when I felt almost like my old self. Yet, the grief was always there below the surface and could be almost paralyzing when it made its way out. No one but Tyger and I truly knew how deeply connected we were in this life, how much in love, and how completely lost we could get in each other. The longing for those private, intimate moments when no words were needed was something that never goes away.

Discovering our connection had survived his death definitely marked another turning point in my grief journey. It lifted my spirits and inspired me to keep living. It was nice to have the will to live again. Missing him was constant, but believing he was still with me gave me strength. I began to see with my soul and I was anxious to find out what was next. Tyger had given me something to hold onto, something to look forward to, and he had my undivided attention.

CHAPTER TEN
Discovering New Truths

AS THE HOLIDAY SEASON APPROACHED, I had no idea how I'd get through it. The weather seemed to be affecting my moods. Sunny days were definitely easier than cloudy ones and I wasn't looking forward to the gray days of late fall and winter.

Tyger had come over to my house for Thanksgiving dinner for the past three years. How would it be without him here? He would always eat, and then I'd pack up plenty of food for him to take home. This year, I was planning to use the fancy dishes he inspired me to buy. My apartment was in an old house just as his was and I also had a built-in hutch. I never owned a set of "good dishes," so I had my small collection of ceramic bird houses in my hutch. One day, he asked why I didn't have dishes in there and after seeing how nice his looked, I started wondering the same thing. Off I went to the Christmas Tree Shop (because I absolutely love a bargain) and found a pretty pattern for much less money than Tyger had spent on his. I set mine up and called him to come see. He stood there looking at it and said, "Wow, you found those at the Christmas Tree Shop? Very nice." All the while he had me in that playful headlock, his usual reaction when he felt my decor looked better than his. I told him from now on I would stand in another room when he came to see something new I'd done to my place.

A few days later, he stopped by to give me a set of battery-operated candles to put on the shelves like he had done with his. He asked if I'd bought extra place settings so I wouldn't need to remove the ones on display for meals or special occasions. His thinking was I'd enjoy my dinner more if I didn't have to disturb the beautiful set up in my hutch. Since I'd purchased about every piece they had in stock at the local store, he brought me to a Christmas Tree Shop in a different town to pick up the extra pieces. His idea worked perfectly and my boys, Sophia, and I enjoyed our Thanksgiving. I clearly felt Tyger's influence as I sat there admiring the plates on display which matched the ones on the table.

He was with me. I could feel him.

I began noticing a specific time quite often. It was 11:11 and it could be a.m. or p.m., I always seemed to catch this time on the clock. After several days of seeing this, I started to wonder if it was Tyger trying to get my attention.

I mentioned this to a friend of mine who was intuitive and she said she needed to think about it. She got back to me the next day and asked if I was having any trouble with my car. Something about my car was coming through strongly for her.

I said, "No, my car is running fine. I do need an oil change, though. I'm a few hundred miles overdue."

She told me I should take it in for an oil change and have them check everything thoroughly. The following Saturday, I took the car in. While waiting for them to finish, I scrolled through my phone to pass the time. The technician came in and told me the air filter was dirty, and the manufacturer recommends changing it every *blah, blah, blah...* would I like to have this done today? I declined and he said everything checked out fine and he'd be finished in a few minutes. I thanked him and went back to my phone. When I looked down, I gasped, the time was 11:11. I stared at that phone for the entire minute in total disbelief. Wow, it really was him and he was trying to tell me to keep up the maintenance on my car. He was a huge believer in preventative maintenance and his vehicles were well taken care of.

His motto was, "You've got to take care of your car so it'll keep taking care of you."

I felt so loved; that familiar protected feeling I'd known the entire time we were together. He was keeping me on my toes, reminding me of important lessons he'd taught me.

In that moment, I said to him, "Thank you, baby. I'm going to be okay, aren't I? You're going to make sure I'm okay." The time 11:11 continues to play a significant role in my life as well as the number combination 111 or 1111.

Since I was still unemployed, I was becoming quite accustomed to sleeping as late as I wanted. I'd wake up early, decide I wasn't ready to rise yet, roll over and drift back off to sleep. One particular day, when I began to wake up for the second time, I heard music. With my eyes still closed and not quite fully awake, I thought to myself, "What song is that? I know that song." It continued to play, then it hit me, "Oh, that's Frankie Valli singing *My Eyes Adored You.*" But, where was it coming from? It was so clear as I listened to the words: *My eyes adored you... like a million miles away from me you couldn't see how I adored you... so close, so close and yet so far.*

As I became more aware, I opened my eyes and the music faded. *Oh, my goodness. It just happened again.* This time, it was a song I recognized even though I hadn't heard it in many years. I grabbed my phone, found the song on the Internet, and listened to the whole thing. The tears streamed down my face at the beautiful words my love had sent to me. What a perfect song. His eyes really had unmistakable adoration every time he looked at me. Hearing the words to this song, I felt completely wrapped in his love. For those few moments, the loneliness was gone and it was Tyger and me connected through music.

Less than a week later, it happened again. This time, it was the Gap Band's *Outstanding.* I laid there listening to this song in my head as I was waking up and the words were expressing what he wanted me to know: *You light my fire, I feel alive with you baby, You blow my mind, I'm satisfied.* Wow, he was really communicating with me through music and he seemed to be telling me he was alive and proud of how I was doing. The same way he had always encouraged me and lifted me up in this life, he was still doing it from where he was now. Again, I found the song and listened to the whole thing, smiling from ear to ear as the tears fell.

He's with me, he really is with me.

These amazing things were happening and I wanted to shout to the world and tell everyone he was still alive. Unfortunately, not everyone was ready to receive the news. I would mention what was going on and get some reactions that were less than what I'd expected. Either I'd hear someone's religious viewpoint on what occurs when we die or I'd feel a sense of pity.

"Poor Diane. She's so heartbroken she's started imagining things."

Even if they didn't speak those words, their tone of voice and facial expressions said it for them. The look was the same every time. They were smiling, but their eyes sort of glazed over and I'd know it was pointless to continue. It didn't take long for me to learn not everyone was as enthusiastic about my experiences as I was, so I was better off keeping them to myself. I found it contradictory how so many people had offered to help, yet they were quick to let the wind out of my sails when I tried to share this news. I didn't think they intentionally did this to make me feel bad; they simply didn't know any better.

I became highly selective with whom and how much I was willing to share. I wasn't going to let anyone rob me of my happy moments. This was as real to me as any communication I'd had with a person standing right in front of me. Tyger loved all kinds of music, so it made perfect sense he'd choose to communicate in song.

As real as it was and as happy as this contact made me, I still longed for his physical presence. By the next day after having one of these wonderful experiences, I was back to the sadness of missing him. This frightened me as I didn't want him to think I was ungrateful so I'd apologize.

"I'm so sorry, baby. Please don't stop sending messages or think I don't appreciate them. I really do and they make me so happy. I miss you being here physically and I get so sad sometimes. Please understand how hard it is without you here, baby. I love you." My heart felt as though he understood.

I received a call from my goddaughter, Crystal, one day. She was one of the few people I could speak to about my experiences without ever feeling like she was judging me or doubting the validity of what I was telling her. She believed deeply in soul connections and was very spiritual.

Crystal called to tell me I had to listen to a song. Her spirit told her I needed to listen to *Together Again* by Janet Jackson. She said she had no explanation why, all she knew was it was extremely important she get that message to me.

After the phone call, I went to my room, laid on the bed, and listened to the words: *Dream about us together again, what I want is together again baby, I know we'll be together again cause - everywhere I go, every smile I see, I know you are there, smiling back at me.* Silent tears started to fall as I continued to listen: *Dancing in the moonlight, I know you are free because I can see your star shining down on me.*

What a gift. What a priceless treasure this was to me. I was so thankful for every word she sang, but even more incredible to me was the fact that my beautiful goddaughter had listened to her spirit which told her to make the call to me. How often in life do we hear a voice prompting us to do something and we simply ignore it or rationalize it away for one reason or another? Crystal hadn't done that, though. She'd heard it and acted on it. There was no way I could ever repay her for passing that amazing message along to me. It was a moment of much-needed peace and I was very grateful.

Christmas was right around the corner, so I put up the tree and did my usual decorating. I've always loved the holiday season with the shopping and getting the house ready. Every year after the decorating was finished, Tyger would come by to see it and we'd sit on the couch together with only the lights from the tree and my miniature Winter Village on. As I decorated this year, I thought back to when Tyger and I worked at the casino and I'd tell him how much I enjoyed the holiday. He told me he didn't really care about Christmas and all he had was a Charlie Brown tree. When he said that, I pictured a sickly-looking tree he'd probably had for a while. Imagine my surprise when I saw his tree in the original box and it actually had "Charlie Brown Christmas tree" printed on the outside by the manufacturer.

How would I get through this holiday without him?

I replayed previous Christmases. The pink recliner he'd bought for Sophia one year. The bike he'd gotten for Mark. The cash he'd put in a card for Aaron. The thoughtful gifts he'd given me over the years. There was sadness at the thought of not shopping for him or looking for a gift to "wow" him. The year before, I'd gotten him a personalized New England Patriots jersey with his name on the back which he loved it.

Since I wasn't working, my shopping budget was low, but I was still able to get the gifts I wanted for everyone. One day, I was in Sears looking for one of the last items on my list. As I rode down the escalator, a display of throw blankets caught my eye. They were heavy-duty fleece blankets and I spotted one with a tiger on it. Since the beginning of our relationship, I'd started collecting things with tigers on them because of his nickname. I also realized what beautiful, powerful animals they were and developed a love for them.

I walked over and picked up this blanket, noticing they were on sale and reasonably priced. "No, Diane," I told myself. "You're not here to shop for yourself and you don't have much money." So, I put it back, paid for the item I was there for, and left.

For the entire time I was at the mall, I could not stop thinking about the blanket. I kept feeling pushed to go back and get it and I kept telling myself I didn't need it. Finally, I gave in. When I got home, I curled up on the couch in my drafty living room with this super-warm blanket and felt so comfortable. It was Tyger pushing me to get a gift from my love.

Sophia had a dentist visit scheduled the week before the holiday during school hours. Her mom was working, so she asked if I could pick Sophia up from school and bring her to the appointment. When we got in the car, she told me she had a surprise for me and pulled a drawing out of her backpack. She had drawn a picture of Tyger wearing his Boston Red Sox hat and a shirt that also had a "B" on it. He was waving with one hand and had a huge smile on his face. She drew things in the background: her rendition of him sitting at our table having Sunday breakfast, the keyboard she loved, a tracing of her hand with her name written on it, and a few other items. This was well-drawn for a kindergartner and I fell in love with it.

She said, "Nani, I drew this for you because I love you and I wanted to make you happy."

I was shocked that this five-year-old could be in school with so many other things to think about yet her thoughts had turned to him and I. Later, when I got home, I put her drawing in a frame and hung it in my room where I could see it from my bed. I believed this was another gift from him, through her. It was his way of telling me he was always with us.

Christmas came and went. I spent the actual day with my sons. We had dinner at home and then, we went and visited with Tyger's family. Later that evening, we spent time with our family at a cousin's house. It was a good day filled with family and love and I was thankful to have gotten through the season.

Tyger found ways to come through and make his presence felt.

Ever since my boys were little, we've had a tradition of sharing a toast of sparkling cider at midnight on New Years' Eve. Aaron was working, so Markie and I had our toast, hugged, and wished each other a Happy New Year. He went back to his room and I stayed up watching TV. Sadness began to well up in me at the thought of starting this New Year without my love. The end of 2014 marked the last year Tyger was physically alive. My heart was in such pain at the thought of him not seeing the new year and having to experience it without him. I hadn't been prepared for my reaction, but it was intense and I cried until I finally fell asleep.

The day after New Year's, I was driving through town when a thought entered my mind out of nowhere.

"I'm cutting my hair."

Almost immediately I answered this thought with, "Yes, yes I am!"

As soon as I walked into the house, I grabbed my laptop and searched for mid-length hairstyles. I found one I liked and the next day, I called a friend who owns a salon and made an appointment. I told no one I was doing this. It was something I needed to do from the moment the thought first entered my mind.

Months earlier, when I decided I was leaving the casino and ending my career in food service, one of the first things I'd said to Tyger was, "Now I can be a girl. I'm getting my hair and nails done and when I find another job it'll be in an office where I can wear my hair any way I want."

I was excited about this idea and so was he. All those years of having to wear my hair up or pulled back with a hat on would be a thing of the past.

When Tyger passed away, any thoughts of going through with my plan left with him. The last thing I thought about was how I looked. I hadn't even worn make-up in months. Yet, here was this thought... something that came suddenly and I instantly knew it was the right thing to do.

I had it done and absolutely loved it. Friends and family thought it looked great and commented on what a huge step it was. There was no doubt of who was behind my much-needed push. It was Tyger's way of telling me it was a new year and time to make some changes.

He'd sent enough signs to convince me he was still with me and now he needed me to trust his direction. In physical life, he hadn't been big on dwelling on things, so I was sure my grief was difficult for him to watch. Never had he wanted to cause me pain; my happiness was always a priority. I believed this was his way of helping me take a step in the right direction. The pain of missing him remained, but the reassurance of knowing he was with me was giving me strength.

I continued to participate in classes through the Department of Labor as required. I was excited about the opportunity to begin free online courses. My status as a "displaced worker" qualified me for the program, so I was taking advantage of every opportunity. Although my world had been devastated by Tyger's passing, the fact remained I would need a job eventually. The program entitled me to ninety days of either business or medical courses. If at least thirty hours were completed within the first ninety days, I could request an additional ninety days at no cost. Since my plan when I left the casino was to completely reinvent myself, this seemed like a great step toward achieving that goal. Initially, I wanted to pursue a career in medical billing and coding, but was told there may not be a high demand in that field. So, I planned to try for an administrative position in a medical office.

I decided to take the business courses first and I dove in head first. Although I already had strong administrative skills from my years in management, I wanted to fine tune them. I was given a license with a password for the courses so I was able to complete them at home. My bedroom became a make-shift classroom and I would shut myself in there for hours at a time. I completed well over the required thirty hours in my first ninety days, so I requested the additional ninety days in order to take the medical courses. My request was granted, so I began with Anatomy and Physiology.

The first bodily system I studied was the cardiovascular system. Due to the way Tyger had passed, I wanted to know the workings of the heart. I realized it wouldn't bring him back, but I had a need to understand how the heart works. I found it fascinating and ended up taking more than one course on the subject, as well as studying the other systems of the human body.

During this time, I also attended workshops on rewriting my resume. Since I intended to change careers, I worked with an advisor who helped me identify the transferable skills I had acquired from my years in food service management. Once my resume had been critiqued by a professional resume writer, I began officially applying to jobs that were of interest. They weren't all medical in nature. There were some that were general office positions. Even as I was applying, I knew that really wasn't what I wanted to do. Still, the clock was ticking and my income had stopped. I was living off of the small amount of money I had in the bank which wouldn't last too much longer.

At this point, I should've been feeling nervous, yet I was strangely calm. I knew I had no money coming in and what was in the bank was getting lower with each month's bills. However, I felt no sense of panic. I maintained my faith in God that there was a job that would be perfect and hand-picked for me.

Each time I applied for a position, I would pray before clicking the "submit" button, "God, I thank you if this is the job you have for me. If it isn't, then I won't be discouraged. I'll know you have something better."

My life began to feel like a constant job search. I had links to the major career search websites on my phone and every time I received a notification of a position that fit my criteria, I'd apply. I repeated my prayer before submitting my resume. Even though time passed, there was still no sense of panic which was beginning to seem strange to me.

Shouldn't I be very worried right now?

That was what I was thinking, but still I was calm.

One day, at a routine visit, I told my doctor about my job search efforts and how I wanted to work in a medical office, but hadn't been able to even get an interview. She offered to introduce me to the office manager, suggesting maybe she could give me some pointers on how to get into the field. When the doctor introduced us, I was shocked to find out the office manager was my cousin. She wasn't someone I had regular contact with, so I had no idea she worked there. We spoke about my situation, how I'd spent twenty years at my last job and had all these transferable skills, but my resume wasn't getting me anywhere.

She said, "Send me your resume. I'll talk to a few people I know in the area and see if anyone is looking for help. We'll find you something."

I was so grateful and thanked her for her willingness to help.

When I got home that afternoon, I debated whether or not to send my resume. She'd probably only made the offer to be nice since I'd shown up unexpectedly. After some thought, I decided to send it. After all, *what did I have to lose?*

Two days later, she emailed me back and said a friend who was an office manager was looking for a front desk person at an office less than ten minutes from my house. The practice had recently been acquired by a large university hospital, so I would need to apply on the hospital website.

My reaction was, "Wow, there's no way I would've ever heard about this position if she hadn't told me about it."

The hospital was located in another part of the state, so this position wasn't even advertised in my area. I applied and was called in for an interview a few days later which led to a second interview. Both interviews went well, but I had to wait for my references to respond and my background check to clear. Less than a week later, I received a call from the hiring manager offering me the position. She remarked at how rare it was to hear back from references so quickly and there had been no delay in my background check.

Just like that... with one month's worth of bill money left in the bank, I was employed. And, what type of practice would I be working in? Cardiovascular and Cardiology. After all the time I'd spent learning about the cardiovascular system, I was hired to work in an office that specialized in it.

I thanked God profusely for blessing me with this position, for hearing my prayers, and for answering them, far exceeding every expectation I'd had. I also knew it was Tyger who'd kept me calm through this process. He knew I would be all right. He was right there working things out in my favor along with our Creator and the Universe.

In the span of nine months, I had undergone major life altering events. I'd left my job only to lose the love of my life unexpectedly just two months later. Losing him had sent me spiraling down into the deepest grief and despair I'd ever known. During this same period, I had to actively participate in searching for a new career on days when I truly wanted to lay down and die from the sadness of missing him. Then, the wonderful discovery that he was with me and able to communicate which brought joy, but also some frustrating moments trying to learn this new form of communication. Now, here I was about to start a new career doing something I really wanted to do. In the process, I'd made some amazing discoveries, but there was so much to learn and I was eager to continue learning in this physical world as well as what lies beyond.

CHAPTER ELEVEN
Seeing With the Heart

One of the best feelings in the world is knowing you have someone in your life who genuinely cares about your happiness. Tyger had shown me what it was like to be completely loved and supported in every way. I told him more than once how comforting it was to know he was always there for me. He knew I was capable of taking care of myself, yet he brought so much security into my world through his willingness to help. He was never forceful or controlling in any way. He just knew what needed to be done and he did it.

The things he did for me were done because he genuinely wanted to help, never for what he might get out of it. I'd never had a man like that in my life who made me feel totally safe and protected.

Our relationship developed slowly, one step at a time with no expectations and no demands. Whatever felt right, we went with it and in the process we gained one another's trust. There were no hidden agendas or ulterior motives involved. It was simply two people who'd found happiness with each other and enjoyed being together. We inspired each other to step out of our comfort zones and experience new things. It all happened so subtly that we barely noticed the changes in ourselves, but it was obvious to other people.

The night before I started my job, I wasn't one bit nervous. Here I was, a girl who had always despised change, yet all I felt was excitement at this opportunity. That was a result of being loved by someone who truly appreciated me in every way. Years of being told how amazing I was and how proud he was to have me in his life changed me from the inside out.

As if hearing the words wasn't enough, his eyes told the same story every time he looked at me. I often asked how he could still look at me as though he were seeing me for the first time. He would smile and say, "Because I enjoy what I see."

Being treated with so much love and admiration had a lasting effect and filled me with confidence. I would often tell him what a rare find he was and how I'd never been involved with anyone who had such a wonderful ability to express their love in so many ways. I adored him for every bit of joy he brought into my life. He made me feel like I could do anything and when he left this physical world, I continued to feel that way. Somewhere in my soul, I knew he would still do everything he could to help me. That knowledge was the reason I hadn't panicked when it looked like I would never get an interview. Deep inside, I knew he was involved, shifting and moving things into place so everything would fall in line.

Why would I feel nervous? There was nothing to fear, so I embraced this new opportunity and was ready for it.

From the very first day, this job was a perfect fit. It was completely different from what I'd done before and I enjoyed every aspect of it. The people were helpful and welcoming and I was thrilled to be there.

The person who trained me was someone I felt I could trust right from the start. Her name was Donna and she and I share similar outlooks on life which made it easy for us to connect. I was excited to be there and she was pleased to have someone to lighten the load of a busy front desk.

It wasn't long before I began wondering if she wasn't part of the reason Tyger had led me to work there. I shared with Donna what I'd been through since losing the love of my life and she reacted with such compassion. It was so nice to have someone to talk to who was completely objective. She hadn't known Tyger or me before, so as I shared the history of us, she was able to listen without any preconceived ideas about our pasts. Listening to her perspective on my experiences and what I'd been through since Tyger's passing aided in my healing process. It was nice to have someone to talk to who listened without judging or discrediting the things I was experiencing. I had many family members who were always available for me to talk to, but I wasn't comfortable sharing with them how deeply I believed Tyger was contacting me. Most of the time, their reactions felt like they were listening, but didn't really believe the way I did. Not only was I doing a job I thoroughly enjoyed, I had found a friend I could confide in about the ways Tyger and I were connected. This was something I desperately needed.

My days were filled with new experiences and interacting with various people. My nights were another story entirely and continued to be trying. In my home life, there was a huge emptiness. Despite how grateful I was for the communications from Tyger and the knowledge he was with me, the physical connection was missing and I longed for that. When he made his transition and passed on, life became unfamiliar to me and my world was shattered. When the pieces landed, they were totally rearranged. My focus and priorities were shifted. What once was big now seemed small and the little things were now huge. I was beginning to see again, but my view had changed. I could never go back to the person I was before, yet, at the same time, I was learning a new way to live. His death sparked an evolution in my soul and I was so grateful he was close by, helping me along on my journey.

It became clear to me there would be no end, no "getting to the other side" of this thing called grief. It would continue to reshape and redefine me. The person I had been before was gone and I had become less, yet more at the same time. There aren't any words to fully describe the experience of physically losing the person who brought pure joy into your life. It's something that has to be felt to be understood.

Through my continued reading about near-death experiences and the effect they'd had on the lives of those who'd had them, I discovered I no longer feared death. I believed and understood there was no "end" to us. We were eternal. Yes, the physical body, these vessels that house our spirits must die someday, but the soul, or the true "self," lives on. As I read more, I felt a change happening within me similar to what occurs after someone returns from one of these experiences. I began seeing how important it was that we really loved ourselves. We had to take the time to do things we enjoyed. The only way to be able to truly love others had to begin with a genuine self-love.

As I came to these realizations, I was amazed this was exactly what Tyger had pushed me to do way back in the beginning of our relationship. To take time for me—Diane time—and how important it was to just "do Diane." These were lessons he had taught me and had given me the tools I needed. I had already begun living this way.

Reading about these experiences only affirmed what he'd shown me. Everything had come full circle and it was liberating when I realized what others thought of me didn't matter one bit. This was my journey and I could do it my way. It was as if my soul was awakening to its purpose as I allowed my spirit to guide me. Looking at life through spiritual eyes allowed me to see with a clarity I'd never known. My love had already progressed in his journey and was guiding me. It was a paradox to be painfully aware of his physical absence, but at the same time feeling so alive in this new knowledge.

Starting a new job and stepping back into the real world gave my life a routine again. A structure that had been missing from being unemployed for all those months. Suddenly, days off had meaning and were something to look forward to. On Mother's Day, the weather was unseasonably warm. I had nothing planned and was trying to decide between getting my laundry started or cleaning the house. All of a sudden, I heard the voice in my head say, "Go to the beach."

My initial reaction was, "Where did that come from?"

I didn't fight it, though. In the next few minutes, I packed a bag and was heading off to the beach. As I got closer, I worried about how I'd feel when I got there. After all, I hadn't been back since Tyger had passed away and I was afraid of what it would be like not being able to text or call him. Would it be too hard? There was only one way to find out, so I paid the parking fee, got a spot on the sand, and laid in the sun. The tears fell as I thought back to my joy the summer before, the texting back and forth, and Tyger's happiness that I was enjoying myself.

Even through the sadness of missing him, though, it was good to be back there and I felt a sense of peace. That beach day showed me I was ready and I could handle it. A few weeks later, I bought a season pass and spent my weekends by the water. I was thankful for the push Tyger had given me on Mother's Day.

With the warmer weather, I noticed when I entered my room after working all day, it smelled like him. The boxes with his clothes in them emitted his scent and I loved that. To open my bedroom door and be greeting by "him" was like being wrapped in a giant hug. I was so grateful for the comfort that brought to my heart each day. Missing him was constant, but being able to smell him in the air didn't add to my pain in any way. I would step into the room and smile, it made me feel as though he'd been there a few moments before I'd arrived. It brought a feeling of much-needed peace to my heart and made our connection that much more real to me.

As I became more open to Tyger's communications, he found more ways to let me know he was with me. I continued to see the time 11:11, but then I began seeing license plates with 1111 or 111.

The first time it happened was after a day at the beach. I had visited the cemetery on my way home and as I was leaving, a thought came to me, "I should stop and pick up some wine coolers."

Tyger knew I enjoyed these so every so often he would buy me a case. I had finished the last of what he'd given me and didn't have any more at home. For some reason, I suddenly had the idea to pick some up. As I slowed down for the red light up ahead, I noticed the license plate on the car in front of me had the numbers 1111 in it. I smiled to myself, knowing it was Tyger letting me know he was with me. He was glad to see me doing what brought me joy. The next week, as I was leaving to go to the beach, the car in front of me had 111 in the license plate. On the ride home that afternoon, as I was merging onto the highway, I ended up behind another car with the same number combination. The following week, in almost the exact same location on the highway, there was another license plate with 111. My heart knew it was him sending these signs to encourage me, to tell me to keep going, and to keep living.

Even through the pain of missing him, there was still room in my life for smiles and laughter. This was the message he sent to me and it made perfect sense. My happiness was always so important to him in this life, so, of course, it would continue to be in the next.

At work one day, Donna and I were talking about how the humidity was bad for our hair. She had a funny picture on her phone of a cat with its fur standing on end and we laughed about how we must look on humid days. She started to walk away then turned back and brought up another picture. It was a yellow chick standing in a police lineup. On either side of it were several yellow marshmallow Peeps. Above the chick's head was a thought bubble that said, "Oh, this is bullshit!"

We laughed and I said to her, "I've seen that before. Someone sent it to Tyger in a text, and he must've thought it was funny so he kept it."

When I got home that night, I found the picture on his phone and decided to bring it to work so she'd see it was the same one. The next day, she told me she had only planned to show me the first picture, but something told her to share that one, too. We wondered if maybe Tyger had urged her to let me see it.

I said to her, "I wonder how long this has been in his phone." I scrolled back to check. As soon as I did, my heart nearly stopped. It wasn't the date that caught my attention, it was the time he'd received it: 11:11am! I grabbed her arm to steady myself because my knees buckled when I saw that time. There was no one who would ever convince me that wasn't a sign from him. Both of us had tears in our eyes because it was such an amazing moment. She'd had no intention of even sharing that picture with me but something in her told her to do it. He had taken that opportunity to prove to me he was with me and wanted there to be a witness so I couldn't explain it away. Donna and I began calling these occurrences "wow moments."

Tyger had more to come.

A year or so before I began my new job, there was a physician who had left the practice. His name was Dr. Bentley and once in a while, we would still get a call from someone asking to speak to him. We would explain he was no longer with us and provide the telephone number to his current office. One particular morning, it was busy and we had many patients. The phones rang constantly. I answered a call and the person asked to speak to Dr. Bentley. I gave them his number and when I hung up, I looked at Tyger's picture which was directly in front of me on my desk and thought to myself, "I wouldn't mind the ringing phones so much if every call was for Dr. Bentley." It was merely a thought I shared with him and I continued working.

The next call I answered was someone asking to speak to Dr. Bentley. This was followed by two more calls asking for him, as well. I smiled at Tyger's picture and knew this was his doing. He'd heard me and was letting me know. I shared this with Donna and a short time later, she took a call and I heard her giving Dr. Bentley's information. We leaned back in our chairs and smiled at each other, both of us knowing who was behind all of it.

The first call I took after lunch that afternoon was once again for Dr. Bentley. Oh, but Tyger wasn't done yet. Several times a week, the staff ordered lunch from a local restaurant. They normally left the money with Donna, since she sits at the first window and pays the delivery person. A few days after the incident with the phone calls, she had stepped away from her window and I noticed a delivery person coming in with food. I went to her window to take the bag and was looking for the envelope to pay them.

The driver said, "This is paid for. It was put on the account." I accepted the food and as I turned to walk away, I looked at the receipt and it was for Dr. Bentley. I nearly collapsed on the floor when I read his name. By then, Donna had come back and we were both overcome with shock, laughter, surprise, you name it. I ran outside and explained it had been delivered to the wrong office. There were people who would say that was nothing more than coincidence, but it absolutely was not. That was Tyger and it was another "Wow" moment.

As my Facebook posts continued, people began suggesting I write a book. This was not something I'd ever considered doing. As I've said before, I was only writing because it was an outlet and it helped me. As time went on, I continued being urged to author a book and it was coming from many different sources. People I'd known all my life, people I hadn't known long at all, a lady I'd met at church, etc. It happened enough to make me stop and take notice. I began to wonder if there wasn't some truth to what they were saying. Maybe they weren't simply being nice. Maybe this was something I was supposed to do in order to help someone else. I was certainly aware of the pain I was living with and the peace I'd found in reading about the experiences of others.

One morning, while I was getting ready for work and speaking out loud to Tyger, I came right out and asked him, "Is this what I'm supposed to do, baby? Am I supposed to write a book? I wish you could send me a sign to let me know. It would be great if the sign could come from Donna."

That was all I said and left for work.

When I got there, I didn't see Donna right away. I sat at my desk and as I logged on to my computer, she walked up and said, "I brought this in for you. It's a book I think you'll enjoy reading."

Wait, what did she just say? Really? A book?

There it was. Tyger's answer to my question, loud and clear. The book she handed me was *Dying to be Me* by Anita Moorjani. She was right; I enjoyed reading it, but it was also an unmistakable sign from Tyger that this was what I was supposed to do. I had no idea how to even begin, though, so I accepted his answer even though I didn't act on it right away. However, writing a book was something I would do someday.

Quite often, I would find myself thinking back to past events and discovering new meaning in them. So many times, Tyger and I would be laying together talking, laughing, enjoying each other and I distinctly remember focusing on even the tiniest detail. I was so happy and felt so loved, I honestly tried to burn it into my memory. He'd leave the room for something and I'd watch him walk out and back in, studying the way he moved. Paying close attention because I never wanted to forget how those moments made me feel. I was completely head over heels in love with a man who loved me back fiercely. This was also something I did while we were riding in the car. We'd be holding hands and he'd lift mine up to his lips and kiss it gently. As he drove I would look over and concentrate on my overwhelming love for him.

Another time we were going out to eat. It wasn't anything fancy, just Chili's, which was my favorite. I had been at the beach all day, so I'd planned to take a shower and throw on a pair of shorts and a top then head out. For some reason, I decided to wear a pretty summer dress, shades of pink and black in a leopard print. It was kind of a long, sleeveless sun dress. The color looked great with the tan I had from my many beach days and even though I knew I was overdressed for dinner at Chili's, it didn't matter. I looked pretty for *him* and he would love it. Before I left to pick him up, I decided to take a few pictures of myself. Now, all these months later, I had the photos I took that day to look at and remember a great night. Was it possible my soul knew how important it was that I remember all those details? As I began to see things with a new clarity, it seemed to me things had been set in motion back then to help me cope with what I was experiencing now.

Then, there was the accident with the deer. As thankful as I was no one had been hurt, it surprised me that we all walked away without a scratch. The car was destroyed and the insurance company counted it as a total loss. Even though Tyger had helped me keep it running and I kept up on preventative maintenance, there was damage done to the undercarriage years earlier which caused rust issues. The car probably didn't have a long future ahead of it. After I received the payout from the insurance company, I was able to buy something much better; a model I had wanted to own since I was younger, but could never afford. I found a used one in great condition that I could buy outright. Months before he passed away, I had been blessed with a more reliable vehicle.

My new way of seeing things assured me none of this had been a coincidence. Everything happened for a reason and there were no mistakes. Things were being put in place then, but I couldn't see it. Even my decision to leave the casino had been a part of what was unfolding. Had I still worked there, it would've meant repeated heartache having to show up there every day after his passing and walk past the area we had spent so much time talking and laughing. Thanks to my decision to leave all those months earlier that was something I never had to experience. In addition, I now had a completely new career and one that I thoroughly enjoyed. Again, there were no mistakes. Things happened as they were supposed to.

My soul awakened to new truths and I embraced them. Although my faith in God, our creator, was and is strong, I felt like I needed to separate myself from the confines of religion. I had gone to church for the spiritual connection and the atmosphere of love had definitely provided that. I cherished the bonds formed during that time and had a deep love and utmost respect for my church family. My beliefs were evolving and expanding beyond what church or religion said was acceptable.

Some of the ideology and practices in the church setting felt man-made and I didn't agree with them. This made it difficult to participate. In no way was I saying that anyone who follows those doctrines was wrong for doing so. I was also not discouraging anyone from attending church or practicing any religion that draws them closer to God or the Source of all that is. The religions of the world have chosen to call this infinite energy of love and light by many names. The name I'm most comfortable with is God. I speak to God daily and He knows my heart better than anyone. I have no doubt of His existence or the love He has for all of us.

My decision to stop attending church was something my spirit needed to do. This was not a separation from God or the relationships I formed with so many wonderful, loving people.

The simple truth behind my decision was we all travel our own paths in this life. What feels right for me might be entirely different for someone else. This is merely a description of my experiences and for me, my road had changed. I still believed strongly in the power of prayer and I spoke to God frequently whether it was about me or on behalf of others. My heart knew prayer was an important part of this life, as well as faith in those prayers being answered. Without a doubt, I knew the prayers of others were what helped carry me through my darkest moments and I understood the power of intercessory prayer.

Although I no longer attended church, that didn't mean my belief in God had diminished or I'd lost touch with my spirituality. In fact, the exact opposite was true; my spiritual connection to the universe had never been stronger. I continued to stand in complete agreement with the core message of what Jesus taught which was to love one another and treat others the way we would like to be treated. I showed love for others because I genuinely felt it, not because it would enhance my experience in the next life. I recognize I was a child of God and a being of love and light. My perspective had begun to change on several things.

First and foremost, I recognized the importance of my own happiness. If something made me feel pressured of caused me stress, I gave myself permission to express those feelings and/or remove myself from the situation. My beliefs were my beliefs and I had the right to express them without concern for who may or may not agree. I respected differences in convictions and expected the same from others.

I felt Tyger with me and recognized the signs he sent me. This new form of communication could be difficult to understand at times, but I was learning more every day. I could never deny they were happening because it wasn't in line with what someone's religion had taught them. Tyger always told me he lived his life by design. Anyone or anything who caused him stress or to lose sleep was removed... simple as that. This became my philosophy, as well, and one of the most important lessons his love had taught me. My life, my journey and my lessons to be learned and I refuse to worry about the approval or judgment of others.

I began to feel a peace I'd never known. A freedom I'd never experienced before. Making choices based solely on what made you happy and what spoke to you on a spiritual level removed the burden of worrying about what others might think. I was changing, evolving, awakening, and allowing myself to embrace every bit of it.

During our years together, Tyger would often say to me, "Thank you, baby, Thank you, Diane, Thank you." He was thanking me for many reasons, for loving him, for allowing him to love me, for bringing new experiences to his life, and for the enjoyment we brought to each other. Now, it was my turn to thank him.

Many nights as I laid in bed staring at our picture I would say to him, "Thank you, baby. So many times you thanked me, but no, thank *you*, for showing me what it means to truly love someone. Thank you for staying with me and finding ways to let me know you're near. Thank you for giving me the confidence to pick myself up again and again and keep pushing.

Thank you for guiding my spirit toward new truths and encouraging me to open my mind and heart. Thank you, baby."

I also realized the relationship we continued to have since Tyger passed was better than some relationships shared by people who sleep in the same bed every night. What an incredible blessing, our love was still strong, intact, uninterrupted and it gave me strength.

CHAPTER TWELVE
Reaching Beyond the Veil

THE DISCOVERY THAT OUR LOVE had survived Tyger's death was an amazing, life-changing experience. It altered the way I thought about every single thing I had ever believed to be true. A whole new world had suddenly been made available to me and I embraced the differences that knowledge brought into my life.

The one thing that didn't change, though, was my relationship status. I did not and do not consider myself to be single. I remain very much in love with the man who opened my eyes to the beauty of what it means to be truly loved in every way. Several months after he passed, I read an article written by a woman who had lost her husband of many years. She titled it, "I'm Married to a Dead Man." In it, she described how she still considered herself married to the man she loved, how his passing from one life to the next didn't mean an end to their relationship.

I read her words, I could relate so closely to everything she said and felt. My love for Tyger hadn't weakened or faded since he had crossed over; it was as strong and real as ever. The messages he continued to send showed our bond hadn't been broken in any way. He was loving me from the other side with the same intensity as he had in this physical world. While I missed being able to touch and feel him, I still had the ability to look at a picture where we were touching and I felt the warmth of his body. My memories of physically touching him were that clear to me.

Around ten months or so after he passed, I spoke to someone I hadn't known for long. I described how hard it was for me sometimes, being here without him. I told her about how often I'd go and sit by his grave and how I speak out loud to him all the time. She listened to me describe these things and then she asked, "Have you dated anyone yet?"

Her words shocked me. Nothing on earth could've been further from my thoughts. Almost instantly I replied, "No! I'm not single! I'm still with him and he's still with me. Why would I be dating?"

At that point, I realized not everyone would be able to understand. There were others who'd said things like that to me. Just days after he died, someone remarked how blessed I was to have found such a deep, true love with him and that "I would find it again someday." My reaction was the same. "No, I won't. No... I absolutely will not."

I've been told by well-meaning friends that the right person would come along and I was too beautiful to be alone. They didn't understand I wasn't alone. Tyger was still with me.

Naturally, there were moments of emptiness without him physically here, but it wasn't about companionship. I was longing for *him*. I wasn't looking to replace him in any way. We were connected on a soul level. Just because I couldn't see him, it didn't mean he wasn't there.

The other thing people have said to me was, "He wouldn't want you to be alone."

My response to that was I wasn't alone. I was surrounded by his love every minute of every day. There had been times at home or when I was driving in the car when I'd suddenly felt his love. A comforting warmth washed over me, almost like being covered with a blanket on a chilly night. It was hard to describe, but when it happened I felt so safe, so peaceful, so loved.

Our relationship before his transition had been like nothing I'd ever experienced. It wasn't as though ours was the only romantic experience I'd ever had, after two marriages and a few other relationships I had plenty to compare it to. With Tyger, though, I had reached the top and the absolute best of everything. He showed his love in every way imaginable and I was appreciated simply for being me. He satisfied needs I hadn't even known I had before and I had done the same for him.

What I was saying was with us there was nothing *missing*. We weren't searching for anything because we had it all in each other. Even though he passed on and went ahead of me into the next stage of this journey, he left me wanting for nothing. He gave it all while he was here and the best part was I got to keep all of that in the same way he got to keep all I gave to him.

There was no unfinished business or next level we hadn't gotten to yet. We'd "gotten it all in" and I was full of his love. It was ingrained in my heart and the depths of my soul. There were no thoughts of my next relationship or starting over with someone else. My mind simply didn't go there. His love was my driving force and what gave me the strength to keep pushing. The gifts he gave me in the way of signs and messages encouraged me and lifted me up when I needed it most.

As it drew closer to the first anniversary of his death, which was also his birthday, I began slipping into a deep sadness. Around two weeks before the day, I suddenly decided to begin working on this book. It had been months since he'd sent the sign that answered my question of whether or not I should write this and it wasn't until just before his birthday/anniversary that I was ready to start. It was as if he knew I needed something to keep me busy and to shift my focus so he nudged me to begin organizing my thoughts and start writing.

I put a lot of thought into the title. I needed something that spoke for both his experience and my own in this journey since his passing. As I walked in the park one day, thinking hard about what to call this book, the title came to me and it fit. He had gone onward into the light and so was I. My soul was awakening to things I'd never even considered before and when his journey began, mine did, as well.

Later that night, I sat and wrote the names of the chapters, to give me an outline of what I wanted to say. Next, I went back to all the posts I'd made on Facebook, the thoughts and feelings I'd shared over the past year. I looked through the notebook I'd kept by my bed and read the letters I'd written to him in the first weeks and months after he passed. It struck me how much material I already had and how much I had to share with the world about our experiences. Was this why I'd felt compelled to keep writing, to keep posting my thoughts? Had he been guiding me even then, knowing this was something we would do? The only answer to those questions was yes, of course.

The weekend after I began writing, I picked up Sophia for her usual weekly sleepover. She told me she had a surprise for me and handed me a drawing. She'd drawn Tyger standing in the rain, holding an umbrella in one hand and a red heart-shaped balloon in the other. She used a blue crayon for the falling raindrops and colored blue puddles on the ground. It was well done and I told her I loved it.

When I asked her to explain it to me she said, "Mike's in the rain with his umbrella. He's bringing you a balloon for your birthday and for Valentine's Day because he loves you."

She went on to point out the puddles and said she'd drawn them because she wanted lots of details. I put the drawing on the table, not sure if I'd find a spot to hang it or not. After all, we already had several drawings she'd done of Mike framed in various rooms of the house. She had even drawn him as a mermaid along with herself, Aaron, Mark, and me. That drawing was so precious and I thought of how Tyger would've laughed to see himself drawn as a mermaid, complete with tail and bikini top. That drawing was one of my favorites so I brought it to work and hung it above my desk. That mermaid family portrait became quite a conversation piece. As I said, I put her latest drawing on the table and in the days that followed, it ended up covered by a growing pile of mail.

I requested the day off from work on the anniversary of Tyger's death. I didn't really have any plans, but I felt it would be best to be free to do whatever I wanted that day. I thought about going to the beach, but then decided to spend a quiet day at home. The only thing I knew for sure was I wanted to buy a few balloons for his birthday and bring them to the cemetery as I sat for a while.

As I began to wake up on the morning of July 30, 2015, there was a soft, almost angelic voice singing quietly in my mind's ear.

Loving you is easy 'cause you're beautiful. And, every day of my life is filled with loving you. It was *Loving You* by Minnie Ripperton. Tyger was reaching out to me and had sent this beautiful song to express how he felt.

As I'd done with the other songs he'd sent, I picked up my phone to find it and listen to all the words. I laid there mesmerized as she sang what he wanted me to know...

Loving you is more than just a dream come true. And everything that I do is out of loving you. Loving you, I see your soul come shining through. And every time that we ooh, I'm more in love with you.

While I listened, the tears fell, slowly at first, and then more and more until I was sobbing heavily. What a wonderful gift he was giving me, letting me know how much he loved me and wanting to comfort my aching heart. I was so thankful, but at the same time, I was overcome with sadness. Exactly one year before, I had woken up so happy and excited to call and wish him a happy birthday. I was full of anticipation for the great day we had ahead of us and looking forward to seeing his reaction when he opened his card and saw his gift. Now, I felt broken, as I stared at his picture on the wall, missing him, drenching my pillow with tears. I told him how sorry I was for feeling that way. He'd sent this beautiful message of love, yet I couldn't get past the sadness of missing his physical presence. Eventually, I cried myself back to sleep.

I slept for a couple of hours and then got up and had breakfast. The tears had stopped, but my heart was heavy in my chest and even my limbs felt like they were weighed down. I thought about doing some writing, but ended up sitting on the couch, blankly staring at the TV. I still planned to go to the cemetery, but didn't seem to have the strength to get up and actually move around.

It was a gray day outside, not raining, but cloudy and it seemed to reflect the way I was feeling. Eventually, I forced myself to get up and get in the car. I stopped and picked up two balloons, one was star-shaped with "Happy Birthday" printed on it and the other was a plain red heart. When I arrived at the cemetery, I got my stool out of the trunk along with the towel I always used to clean his name. I attached the balloons securely to the flower arrangement I had made for him at the beginning of the summer, wiped off his name plate, and then sat there quietly watching the balloons blow back and forth in the breeze.

At last, I spoke, "I'm sorry, baby, for being so quiet. I just don't have anything to say. Today feels like a day to be quiet."

A few minutes later, I heard a car pull up behind me. I turned around and it was a young man who had worked with Tyger and me at the casino. He remembered it was Tyger's birthday/anniversary and had stopped after work to pay his respects. We hugged and I told him how nice it was to see him.

As we talked, another car pulled up and it was a friend who had also worked with us at the casino. Neither one of them knew the other would be there and they never expected to see me. Yet, we'd found ourselves there at the same time and began reminiscing about all the laughs we'd shared with Tyger when we all worked together.

When we talked and laughed, I could actually feel the weight I'd been carrying for most of the day begin to lift. We hugged before they both left and then I turned toward Tyger's grave with a smile and said, "I know that was you. You sent them here to bring me out of that heavy sadness that was weighing me down. You brought us all together to remember the good times and the laughter. Thank you, baby. I love you."

After I got home, I was back to my normal self. I felt peaceful and happy inside. I went into the kitchen and started making dinner. I noticed it had suddenly gotten dark outside. I walked back into the living room and looked out the front window to see it had started raining. And then, it was pouring. Water ran down the hill and there were huge puddles in the parking lot across the street. My heart leaped with excitement as I thought about the drawing my beautiful granddaughter had given me two weeks before. I ran to the table to find it and there Tyger was, standing there in the picture holding his umbrella in the rain with the puddles at his feet. I held the drawing tightly to my chest and went out onto the front porch to watch the rain fall. I have never in all my life been so happy to see rain. This was absolute confirmation for me that he was with us, both Sophia and me, and he had been all along. That drawing was a clear message from him and watching the rain as it fell I was in awe of the power that love possesses. A day that had started with such heartache was ending in pure joy with the realization that love never dies and he was always close and always would be.

In the days that followed, all I did was write. I had to work during the day and afterward I would go to the park to walk. The exercise was doing me good and helping to take off some extra pounds that needed to go. In the evenings, it was writing time until I couldn't keep my eyes open and had to go to bed. Some days I'd be at work with tons of ideas to write about later that night. Then, I'd get home and sit with my laptop open unable to type because the words didn't seem to be flowing.

One morning, after one of those nights, I was in the bathroom getting ready for work. All of a sudden, my mind was overwhelmed with ideas for things I should include in this book. I was curling my hair and a thought would come to me. I didn't want to forget, so I put the curling iron down, ran into my room, and wrote it down. I went back to what I was doing and a few seconds later I had to run back to the notebook to write something else down.

After repeating this four or five times, I finally had to say something. I picked up a picture of Tyger that sits on my bureau and looked him straight in the eye as I spoke, "Okay, baby, I hear you. I know how important it is we get this book written and I know the drive you have to get things done. I promise you we will get this done and it will be great, but right now I *really* have to get ready for work."

My mind seemed to quiet down after that and I was able to finish getting myself together and make it to my job on time.

Tyger was letting me know I wasn't alone in this and there were things he wanted to make sure I didn't forget to include. I was amazed by how clearly the words were coming to my mind like he had a direct link into my thoughts.

Several days later, as I awoke to the sound of my alarm, once again there were words to a song repeating in my head. This time, it was *Guilty* by Barbara Streisand and Barry Gibb. I could hear it softly as I got up and began my usual routine.

Midway through the morning, I mentioned to Donna I had been hearing this song quietly in my mind since I opened my eyes and it had never really left. It kept playing, almost like background music until I decided I better look it up on my phone and listen during lunch. I usually ate in my car, with the radio on, getting some fresh air and this day was no different. I found the song on the Internet and held my phone as I listened to the words:

It ought to be illegal, make it a crime to be lonely or sad, you got a reason for living, you battle on with the love you living on... and we got nothing to be guilty of, our love will climb any mountain, near or far - we are, and we never let it end, we are devotion... and we got nothing to be sorry for our love is one in a million, eyes can see that we got a highway to the sky...

Needless to say, the tears fell as I heard those words. What an amazing song to send. I hadn't heard it in decades and even then I wasn't sure if I ever really listened to all the words. It was a song I'd liked and sang along with on the radio back then, but not something I owned in my music collection. Yet, once again, he had chosen something with perfect lyrics and I was amazed.

That night as I spoke to him at bedtime I said, "You amaze me. You amazed me in this life and you still are from the next." I purchased that song and added it to my iPod. I never get tired of hearing the words that came from his heart straight to mine.

It was a difficult thing to be so grateful for the communications, acknowledging every one of them, yet at the same time filled with longing for the physical presence of the person sending the messages. This was something I lived with daily, an ongoing contradiction of being connected, but separated at the same time. There were times I was fearful that my longing for him would cause him to stop reaching out, that he'd misinterpret my sad moments as doubt that he was still with me. So, I spoke to him and explained that although I was aware of how close he was, in this physical plane I lived in I couldn't help but miss him here. My heart felt that he understood and for that reason he continued to communicate to provide comfort to my aching soul. He was creative in his ways of letting me know he was with me.

There was a day I was at the park for some exercise after work. It was a humid August day and I was drenched in sweat. I was wearing an old pair of shorts and a T-shirt with my hair pulled back, frizzy from the humidity. As I walked along, a young man was going the opposite way. He said hello and I said hi and continued moving.

As he passed, he asked, "Has anyone told you today that you're beautiful?"

I answered, "No, but thank you."

Immediately after that, I felt comforted, wrapped in a warm embrace and I knew that was a message from the man I love. He had sent it through this random person, but it was definitely from Tyger and I knew it. I smiled and thanked him for sending those words he'd said to me so often in the past, yet I hadn't heard him say since he left this world.

A week or so later, I was going through the parking lot to my car to have lunch. I was carrying my water bottle and my purse, anxious to get in, open the windows, and take a ride to break up the work day. I noticed a butterfly flying around up ahead of me. All of a sudden, it flew straight towards me and landed directly on top of my water bottle. I was stunned by this because I was moving at the time, yet somehow it landed there, sat for a second or two, and then flew away.

My heart knew it was Tyger saying hello. A quick reminder he was with me always. My spirit was instantly lifted and my heart filled with love. What an incredible experience that was. In all my years, I had never had a butterfly land anywhere on me or anything I was carrying. Yet, somehow this had happened and while I was in motion. There was no mistaking this for anything but a direct communication from Tyger and I thanked him for the wonderful gift.

With all of this happening, I began to feel like it was time to contact a medium and have a one-on-one reading. It felt as though it was time. His communications were coming through so clearly and I wanted something more direct.

A friend told me about a medium, Laura, she'd been to who was very good and had done an amazing reading for her. She gave me her number and I called to set up an appointment.

For a few days, we seemed to be playing phone tag, leaving messages for one another, but unable to connect. Finally, I was able to reach her and we scheduled an appointment. Our conversation was short. She mentioned a day and time and I said that would work for me. I didn't tell her anything about myself or how I'd gotten her number and she asked no questions. I made the appointment for as late in the day as possible because of my work schedule, but I was still concerned I might be late. There were days I stayed past my shift because the doctors sometimes ran behind and I had to wait to check out the last patient. I asked for permission to leave exactly at my scheduled time that day and was told I could as long as I informed the doctors. Even still, I was worried I'd end up having to stay late and would miss my appointment time. For several days, I thought about this and it was causing stress.

Then, five days before my reading, Donna told me she was asked to work a Saturday but wasn't able to do it. All of a sudden, it was like a light bulb lit up above my head. If I were to work that Saturday, I would have to take a different day off in that same week. I could negotiate a way to get the day of my reading off and then I wouldn't need to stress about making it there on time.

I let my manager know I was available to work that Saturday if I could have Tuesday off. She approved it and just like that, my worries were over.

I thought to myself, "Tyger was probably laughing the whole time I was worried about being late. He knew it would all work out." This was a sign to me of how important it was for me to have this reading. As badly as I wanted to hear directly from

Tyger, he wanted to speak to me, as well. This was going to be something I'd never forget. I knew that at the deepest level of my soul.

Several times over the years, Tyger and I had spoken about confirmation of things. There was a day I had just arrived at the casino, back when we still worked there. As I passed a guy who was sitting on a bench, he said to me, "You are so beautiful,"

I thanked him, but it surprised me to hear this so early in the morning from a complete stranger.

A short time later, I mentioned this to Tyger and he said, "See? That's confirmation. I tell you all the time how beautiful you are, so there you go."

He often told me he wasn't really well-known around town. His exact words were, "Many people know *of* me, but not too many actually *know* me."

I told him that couldn't be true; everyone knew him, but he insisted they really didn't. While I was helping to promote one of the events he was producing, I talked to a lady who'd grown up in our town and I mentioned Tyger's event. Her response surprised me.

She said, "I don't know Tyger. I know his brothers and sisters and I've heard his name for years, but I don't know him."

I went back and told him what she'd said. His exact words were, "There's that confirmation again. I told you people don't know me."

As I prepared for this upcoming reading, I felt I needed to explain to him why I was doing it. One night, as I spoke out loud to him, I said, "Baby, please don't think by going to this medium I'm doubting you're with me. I know you are and I recognize the signs you send. I just need this confirmation. The same confirmation we spoke of many times. That's the reason I'm doing this and I know you understand."

My appointment was scheduled for a Tuesday at 6:00 p.m. Leaving work at 5:30 p.m. on Monday, all I could think of was what I'd be experiencing twenty-four hours later. I was excited but guarded at the same time. I went directly to the cemetery, got my stool out, and sat down to talk with my love. I asked him to please be there, to please come through and give me the confirmation I so desperately needed. Again, I explained my reasons for doing this and told him how badly I needed to know he was with me.

That night, at bedtime, I wrote down some questions I would ask during the reading:

1. *Are you okay there? Happy?*
2. *Could you see what was happening moments after your death?*
3. *Do you hear me when I speak to you?*
4. *Am I on the right path in life?*
5. *Are you with me often?*
6. *Am I missing signs from you?*
7. *Can you describe what it's like where you are?*
8. *Did you keep all your memories?*
9. *Did you give Sophia the idea to draw the picture of you in the rain?*

When I finished writing the questions down, I spoke to his picture as I did every night, said my prayers, and then drifted off to sleep.

In the two weeks leading up to this day, I was excited about connecting with him. Now that it would be taking place the next day, my anticipation had turned to nervous apprehension, I was afraid of being disappointed again.

CHAPTER THIRTEEN
A Spiritual Connection

I WOKE UP EARLY, about the usual time I'd normally get up on a work day. Even without an alarm my eyes always seemed to pop open at the same time. Immediately, I began recalling the dream I'd had as I slept.

I dreamed of Tyger. He was alive and sitting outside in front of his house. There was a woman next to him and every time I would speak to him, she would respond. No matter what I said, he refused to answer. I left and tried calling his phone, but no luck there either. I sent text after text with no reply. In the dream, I felt such pain, *why won't he speak to me? I know he can hear me, why doesn't he answer?*

As I laid there thinking about this very unpleasant dream, I began to hear music softly in my mind:

You are the sunshine of my life, that's why I'll always be around. You are the apple of my eye, forever you'll stay in my heart.

Stevie Wonder's song. I knew instantly Tyger had sent that. He wanted me to hear those words as he was trying to reassure me. My dream seemed to be an expression of my fear that he wouldn't come through during this reading. Even though I fully acknowledged the beautiful song he'd just sent me, there was still doubt about what I would hear later that day.

I got up and went to the park to clear my mind. From there, I went back to the cemetery. As I spoke with him, I suddenly broke down in tears, explaining once again how badly I needed confirmation and how much I needed to connect.

I arrived for my appointment a few minutes early. Laura greeted me at the door and as soon as I saw her face I knew I would be comfortable with her. She had a welcoming aura about her which made me relax. She walked ahead of me as we entered her office and then she turned and said, "I need to shake your hand. I normally don't do this. I wait until we sit down to touch your hand because that's how I connect. For some reason, though, I need to shake your hand."

As we took our seats, she told me to place my purse on the opposite side of my chair, furthest away from her. This was so she didn't pick up on or read from things I might have inside. I was so excited to be there that I didn't even think about taking out the notebook with my questions.

She began with a prayer to her spirit guides with her hand over mine. Midway through her prayer, her voice seemed to get stuck in her throat for a second, almost like a slight gasp and then she finished the prayer. She began by speaking to me about my job, telling me there was a change. She saw a transition for me in my career. I confirmed I had recently changed careers and she went on to discuss things she saw happening for me and I would have a successful future there.

Next, she asked, "Who is the man with you?"

I was shocked by her question which I was sure she saw in my expression.

Again she asked, "Who is the man with you?"

I said, "Well, it must be the love of my life."

That was all I said.

I didn't tell her he had passed away or anything else about him. From that point on and for the better part of an hour, I would hear things that forever changed the way I looked at life:

Laura: He's very talkative for a man. He has a lot to say. He was with you from the time you walked in. I picked up on him immediately. That's the reason I had to shake your hand. He was coming through as I said my prayer which is why I gasped. Did you hear me gasp during the prayer?

Diane: Yes, I did hear that. *I began to feel happiness welling up in me, from deep inside. He's with us, I just know it.*

Laura: He tells me he loves you. He loves you inside and out. He loves you so much and you make him very happy. He says you're perfect like a dessert to him. He keeps showing me a dessert and telling me this is you. Do you understand this?

Diane: Yes I do. He called me his "Cherry on Top." *At this point, the tears are flowing.*

Laura: He keeps repeating that he loves you. He loves you so much. You're a good girl and he loves you. He chose you. You're the one. He's showing me the moon and stars. He keeps showing this over and over. Does this make sense to you? Did the two of you look at the moon and stars?

Diane: No, we never did that. But, earlier today I was changing my cover photo on my Facebook page and I searched for a picture of a tiger with the moon and stars. I found an image and that's my new cover photo. *Wait... was he right there with me while I searched for that picture?*

Laura: He wants you to celebrate. He always wants you to celebrate. Any occasion that calls for celebration. That's what he wants you to do. Always celebrate. Have you stopped celebrating? Is that why he's telling you this?

Diane: Mmm... I guess. I did celebrate the holidays, though, and got balloons for his birthday that just passed. Not really sure why he's putting so much emphasis on this.

Laura: I don't know, but he keeps saying he wants you to celebrate.

Diane: [thinking to myself] *Earlier today during my walk, I was listening to a song called "Let's Celebrate" and I replayed it several times. When I got home, I shared the song on Facebook as a dedication to him, saying I would always celebrate our love. He was there. He was with me and that was why he keeps using the word "celebrate." He was telling me he was there!*

Laura: He's talking about the 911 call. He says there wasn't time. There still wouldn't have been enough time. He wants to make sure you know that there wouldn't have been enough time. Do you understand?

Diane: Yes, when he began having difficulty breathing, I asked if he wanted to go to the Emergency Room. He shouted, "No," so, I waited a couple of minutes and then looked again and he was in worse condition, telling me to call 911. I've asked myself many times if he would've made it had I called the first time, when he told me not to. *Thank you, baby. Thank you for easing my fears that I could've saved you if I hadn't listened and called sooner.*

Laura: He says no, there wasn't enough time and he still wouldn't have made it. He tells me he ascended immediately. It happened quickly and he was gone from his body. He's telling me he had pneumonia previously and they treated him with antibiotics or steroids.

Diane: Yes, he did have pneumonia less than a year before he passed. *Wow, no way she could possibly have known that unless he had told her.*

Laura: He's showing me that this experience was the same as pneumonia. There was distress in his lungs; one more than the other. He shows me problems with blood pressure, sugar, cholesterol. He wishes he'd walked more and ate better. He was eating too much, he knows that now. He keeps repeating "100 pounds, 100 pounds." Do you know what this means?

Diane: Yes. After his bout with pneumonia and being in the hospital, he told me he wanted to lose 100 pounds, which was his goal. *Oh, my goodness, is this really happening? He's here. He is really here. She had no way of knowing this. I wondered if what he felt the night he passed was the same feeling he'd had with pneumonia. He's telling me it was the same.*

Laura: Your husband is so sorry for leaving the way he did. He thought he'd have more time. He didn't want to leave you alone. He wishes he left you in better shape financially. He should've set you up better. He's sorry there's not more money.

Diane: I understand. My well-being was very important to him and he helped financially even though I never asked. This makes sense to me.

Laura: He loves you inside and out. He loves your body. I feel he really loved your body in this life. He keeps wanting me to reach out to touch you. He loves you inside and out. I feel like he told you this often. He's talking about you being naked. He keeps saying "naked." Did he enjoy watching you undress? Your husband really loves your body, do you understand this?

Diane: Oh yes, he told me constantly how he enjoyed looking at me. I used to ask how he could still look at me as though he was seeing me for the first time and he'd say because he liked what he saw. *Really, baby? I can't believe you're telling this woman about me being naked. You always wanted me naked. Remember when you told me if we lived together, you'd have me doing everything naked, cooking, cleaning, etc.? I've never shared that with anyone. You're here, baby. You're really right here.*

Laura: He says you make him so happy. You made him feel things he thought he wasn't capable of feeling. He's holding out a ring, a wedding band, saying he loves you.

Diane: Actually, we weren't married.

Laura: Oh, I'm sorry, but he comes through as a husband. The connection is so strong between you two. Again, he's telling me, "She's the one. I chose her. She's my girl." He wants me to tell you there is no goodbye, only hello. He says you will see each other again and he'll be there to take your hand. He's sorry the two of you never got to dance together. That's the first thing you'll do when you meet again. He wants to dance with you.

Diane: [smiling] That's true. We never once danced together. *I feel you, baby. I feel you right here with us.*

Laura: He says it will be a long time, though. You will be here in this life for a long while. He tells me the first three months after he passed, you wanted to leave this life to go with him. Do you understand this?

Diane: Yes, I kept asking God to take me. I didn't want to stay here without him it hurt too badly. I wanted my physical life to end so I could be with him. *Right after he passed, I told him he better be the first one to greet me when it was my time to go. I want him right there, ready to take my hand. He heard me say that and now he's telling me he will be there. Wow...*

Laura: He's telling you no, you can't go there right now. It's your time to be here in this life. He's with you, though. He says he sends you signs and hears everything you say to him. He tucks you in at night and he wants you to keep listening to the music, keep listening to the songs. Just keep listening to the music.

Diane: I don't understand. Music?

Laura: Yes, he says keep listening. Just remember I said that, okay? The meaning may come to you later. Who is Michael?

Diane: He is. His name is Michael.

Laura: Oh, I see. He kept telling me to say, "Michael, say Michael." I normally don't say the name Michael during readings because that's my husband's name and I don't want to confuse readings. He was insisting I say it, though, so I did.

Diane: [To myself] *Just like my baby, "Say it, just say it." I could imagine him telling her that.*

Laura: Tell me about the forehead kisses. He's showing me kisses on the forehead or top of the head. Do you understand this?

Diane: Yes, I always kissed the top of his head when he sat on the side of the bed. Before I left, I would stand in front of him in his arms and kiss the top of his head.

Laura: He's showing me coffee, what's this all about?

Diane: Coffee was our "thing." One of the first questions we asked each other during our morning call was "Have you had a coffee yet?" He gave me a Keurig for Christmas and I bought him one for his birthday. *You still remember our coffee, baby?*

Laura: Someone drank wine. He's showing me wine or something like that in a bottle. Do you understand this?

Diane: Yes, he always bought me wine coolers. He would go to BJ's and buy cases for me.

Laura: He's talking about his dad now. He says you saw him recently?

Diane: Yes, I did. I saw him last weekend. *Wow, baby. You were right there with us.*

Laura: He's telling me you are close to his family. You have contact with two family members more than the rest. Do you understand this?

Diane: Yes, he must mean his sister and niece. I speak to them often.

Laura: He sees that and it makes him happy. He wants you to know it makes him very happy. He's showing me plane tickets, he wants you to go and have a good time and enjoy yourself. Are you planning a trip?

Diane: Yes, I'm going to Las Vegas in the spring with my cousins. Just the girls are going and we just started checking airline prices.

Laura: He wants you to go. He really wants you to travel, have fun, and be happy. He's talking about your laugh. He wants you to laugh again. It's hard seeing you sad and somber.

Diane: I'm trying. I'm starting to find my smile again.

Laura: He says to tell you God is good. He's happy where he is now and it's better than he ever imagined. He keeps saying, "You were right. God is good." He describes where he is as a "white banquet." Those are the words he's using. White linens and white curtains. Glass and crystal and everything sparkles with light. He says it feels cozy there. Cozy is the word he's using to describe it. He compares looking at this world to looking through a two-way mirror. He can see you, but you can't see him. He says that's what it's like. He's telling me you look nice. He says you look really nice, but you always look nice. What is this about? Did you buy new clothes or something?

Diane: No, but I lost weight... about twelve pounds. *I'm so glad you're okay, baby. I'm so relieved to know you're happy and in a beautiful place. I wonder all the time what it's like where you are. Thank you, baby.*

Laura: Well, that's what he means then, but he says you always look nice. Always good, he says, always good. Tell me about the children. You both have children. Tell me about them.

Diane: We each have two.

Laura: He's not showing me two and two. He keeps saying three and one, three, and one. Does this make sense to you?

Diane: Not really. We each have two children, my two sons and his son and daughter.

Laura: Oh, I see, three boys and one girl. Now I understand why he says three and one. Tell me about your oldest son. He has babies. Is it three babies?

Diane: Yes, he does have three. *Wow... I never mentioned I was a grandmother.*

Laura: One of them has a darker complexion than the other two?

Diane: Yes, my grandson. *How in the world could she possibly know that?*

Laura: Tell me about the oldest one. You have her on the weekends, right? Every weekend?

Diane: Yes, I do have her every weekend. We are very close.

Laura: [laughing] He's telling me, "Every weekend, every weekend." Does she dance? He says she dances around.

Diane: No, but he did want to sign her up for dance classes. He talked about it before he passed.

Laura: Well, he communicates with her while she's playing. He's whispering to her and she hears him. Pay close attention to anything she tells you.

Diane: I felt strongly this was happening. She speaks of him so often and draws pictures of him all the time. *I knew it, I knew it, I knew it. I knew you were communicating with Soph. She talks about you all the time and you're always in her thoughts. Thank you for staying close to her, baby, thank you.*

Laura: He says for you to keep writing. He loves your words. He really loves your words and doesn't want you to stop writing. Do you understand this?

Diane: [more tears] Yes, I'm writing a book about us and my experiences since his passing. *So glad you approve of what I'm doing. I knew you were involved.*

Laura: He's showing me hearts. He keeps drawing a heart shape over and over. Hearts seems to be very important to him. He's insisting I tell you about this. There's a strong message tied to these hearts. Does this mean something to you?

Diane: Not exactly. I'm not sure what he's trying to say.

Laura: Well, keep that in mind. There's definitely something connected to hearts that he wants you to know. He says again that he loves you. He can't believe you chose him. Did he have a hard time believing you wanted to be with him?

Diane: Yes, he did at first.

Laura: He wants you to know he's always close, he'll keep sending signs to let you know. He wants you to be happy and to know you will be together again.

As the reading came to a close, I showed her the picture Sophia had drawn of him standing in the rain with the umbrella and heart-shaped balloon in his hand. Immediately, she said, "There are several hearts in this drawing," pointing out the hearts Sophia had drawn. As I got up to leave, she asked if I was able to hear him speaking as he was coming through to her. I said I couldn't and she said it almost seemed as if I could because as he told her things, he seemed to think she already knew about them, but she didn't. She wondered if the messages had passed through me first. I told her I wasn't aware of anything like that. I was listening to the messages she passed along. She told me she holds classes on how to better connect in spirit and she thought I'd be a good candidate. I told her I'd be interested in learning more and possibly taking those classes. She thanked me for coming and said she would very much like to read my book when it's finished.

We hugged and I said, "Thank you, God bless you."

Walking to my car with tears in my eyes, I was smiling from ear to ear. I got the confirmation I needed so, so badly. He was with me, he was really, truly with me and I was not imagining any of it.

As I drove, I tried to replay everything she'd said to me. Could I remember everything? Damn it. Why hadn't I asked to record our session or, at least, take notes? I pulled into a parking lot to call Donna. She was the only person who knew I was having a reading and I promised I'd call as soon as it was over. I was still crying when she answered the phone, trying desperately to remember everything I'd heard in the past hour. I remembered some things, but knew I was forgetting a lot. As I kept talking, more and more came back to me.

She was overjoyed at what she heard and she said, "Oh, Diane. There's your validation. You never have to wonder again if you're imagining things because now you know he's always with you. This is so beautiful. You read about things like this, but to know someone who is actually experiencing it is just incredible."

She was so excited for me and I was so grateful to have someone I could share this amazing news with.

This could be a delicate subject and there was nothing worse than having someone completely destroy your happiness by trying to disprove everything you'd just experienced. Unfortunately, I knew that would be the case with many people, some of whom I'd known all my life. Part of me wanted to scream from the highest rooftop, "He's alive, he's still alive!" However, I knew the reaction I'd receive. It saddens me that so many refused to believe there was more to life than what we experienced in this physical world. Everyone had to discover things in their own time and on their own journeys. So much was said during the reading that the medium would have absolutely no way of knowing. Things I'd never spoken about to another living soul, intimate details she relayed to me exactly how they had happened. I'm not sharing all of what was said during the reading because it's too personal and very sacred to me. I will say that the only other person who knew any of those things was Tyger, and as I listened to her repeat what he was saying, I knew beyond any shadow of a doubt that he was there and he was speaking.

As I drove along on the highway, I thought over what he shared during that hour. I thought about what she had told me.

"Keep listening to the music, keep listening to the songs."

All of a sudden it hit me, *he's talking about the songs he sends me, How did I not know that? Oh, my goodness, baby. I know what you were telling me. I'm sorry I didn't get it right away. Yes, yes, yes, of course, I'll keep listening. I knew those songs were coming from you. I just knew it. Every single song had a perfect message attached to it when I listened to the words.*

At this point, I was so full of joy as I drove home on that dark highway. He still loved me the same as he did in this life. Our love was perfect, undisturbed, uninterrupted, and unbroken in any way. No wonder I hadn't lost the feeling of him not letting me fall. He never left. He'd been with me all along and somewhere on a soul level, I'd always known that. I was absolutely in awe of the way life was designed, the illusion of separation that death brought when in truth there was no separation at all. He knew everything I'd experienced since he crossed over. He heard me and he tucked me in at night. He loved me and he was very aware of how much I loved him. Thank you, God. Thank you for allowing this connection and for opening my heart and mind to the realities available to those who believe. I was filled with so much joy and my tears were a mix of gratitude, relief, validation, love, happiness, and comforting peace.

When I got home, I looked at the questions I had brought with me but failed to ask. As I read them, I realized he had answered every single one of them and a few more that were in my heart, but I hadn't written down. *You were right here, weren't you, baby? Right next to me when I wrote those questions and you made sure I got my answers. Even the ones I held deep inside, you knew what I needed to know and you answered.* Absolutely incredible. The experience opened my eyes to truths I'd always hoped for yet didn't quite believe were possible. He wasn't gone; he was just in a different place although very much whole and alive. He remembered all of his experiences here and still had his sense of humor and the best parts of himself.

During the reading, Laura had asked if Tyger swore a lot in this life and I said yes. She said, "He wants me to tell you he's not like that now. That was part of his humanness that was left behind."

The time I spent listening to him speak through her was the most loved I'd felt since the day Tyger had left this physical world. It wasn't an ordinary feeling of being loved, it was a familiar love, *his* love. When I spoke to him at bedtime that night, it was with joy in my heart and a smile on my face. Tears were there also, but it wasn't the usual sad tears. These were cleansing tears and they were washing away the doubt, the fears, the negative thoughts that crept in every once in a while. I was able to close my eyes and as I pulled the covers up around me, I imagined him there, tucking me in as he said he would. One thing about my baby was he was a man of his word. If he said he tucked me in, then that was exactly what he did. I fell into the deepest, sweetest sleep I'd had in a long time.

When I opened my eyes on a new day, there was a song playing softly in my mind:

Love, there's nothing better than love, what in the world could you ever be thinking of. It's better by far, so let yourself reach for that star and go no matter how far to the one you love.

Wow, how beautiful. I'd always loved that song by Luther Vandross and Gregory Hines. I had to find it and listen to every word. I wanted to get his entire message:

Oooh love, wakes me up every day and I thought no one could ever make me feel this way. It fills me up, every time I hear her say, she's still in love and no one could take her love away.

Every verse was better than the one before and I felt my eyes well up as I continued to listen:

...and I mean all these words I say, you don't have to guess what's going on inside my head. Just try to know, all the things that our hearts say. Listen to love and always get love to lead the way.

Yes, indeed, baby. There's nothing better than love. Realizing ours was as strong as ever was something no one could ever take away from me. My brain was finally convinced of what my heart had known all along. We were connected by the most powerful force in the universe and nothing could change that. Not the doubters, the religious, the non-religious or anyone else. Just like you said, "God is good." I believe that now more than ever. He took two imperfect people and knew they'd be perfect for each other... and He was right.

CHAPTER FOURTEEN
Awakened Soul

DISCOVERING THE TRUTH, that he still lived and I hadn't lost him, completely changed me from the inside out. My views on life and our purpose here had been totally transformed and I now saw myself as a spiritual being.

There was a quote I'd read often which said, "We are not human beings having a spiritual experience, we are spiritual beings having a human experience." These words made perfect sense to me. Realizing life continued past physical death and learning about what follows convinced me we were so much more than the bodies we inhabited.

I embraced this way of thinking and it liberated me in many ways. I'd always been a positive thinker, but now I was able to see how damaging negative thoughts and energy really could be. I'd arrived at a place in my life where I'd decided to do what made me happy and to go where my spirit leads me. Being loved by such a wonderful soul and learning that our love remained intact taught me how important it was to live life happy. His love gave me the confidence to do just that. The pain caused by thinking I'd lost him only fueled my conviction to live the way it felt right to me. That meant expressing myself according to my own truths, choosing how to spend my days, refusing to engage in anyone else's negativity, and keeping gratefulness in my heart always. I refused to spend any of my time worrying about what others thought of my beliefs or actions. Although I was still grieving and missing him terribly in the physical, my spirit had gone through a renewal, a rebirth of sorts, and I welcomed this new way of being. This metamorphosis had already begun before we connected through the medium, but once I understood that there was no separation, it proved to me that this really was the only way to live.

Receiving confirmation Tyger was still very much with me lessened the weight of sorrow that had been on my heart since his passing. I knew my grief journey hadn't ended. The sadness of missing his physical presence was a part of me and would be until the day we met again.

One of the messages he shared with me was my time in this life would be long, but, at least, now I had no doubt he was always close. Just knowing he was alive *somewhere* brought me such comfort. Hearing the personal things that came through during the reading strengthened my will to live, to continue on in this life.

On my visit to the cemetery the following day, I said to him, "Thank you, baby. Thank you so much for finding so many ways to let me know it was really you. Yesterday, as I sat here crying, begging you to please come through, you were probably so frustrated with me, knowing full well that you'd be there. No wonder Laura felt your presence as soon as I walked in. Your need to confirm was just as strong as my need for confirmation."

Having all doubt removed of his survival elevated my spirit to another level and boosted my confidence. It took away the second guessing I had done in the past, wondering if everything I considered a sign was actually that. It wasn't only *what* she'd said during the reading that convinced me it was him, it was also *how* she'd said it. I knew the way he spoke, the way he felt, and the way he thought. The emphasis that was put on certain points was absolutely the way he would've spoken if he had been standing right in front of me.

As I sat there listening and taking in what she relayed from him, my heart traveled back to countless conversations the two of us had had while laying together in his bed. The intimacy between us had always been far beyond what either of us had ever known and that came through so clearly. In physical life, he never held back his feelings for me or the intensity of his attraction to me. He expressed his thoughts and feelings verbally and non-verbally, every chance he got. So, to sit there with this stranger and hear the same sentiments relayed to me with equal intensity... those words went directly to my heart, to the place reserved only for him.

During the reading, Laura had also mentioned a necklace. She said Tyger was showing her a necklace and she asked if I knew what that was about. I told her I was wearing all of the Alex and Ani bracelets he'd given me, but he'd never given me a necklace.

She said, "No, he's definitely showing me a necklace."

I thought about it, but couldn't get what he was trying to say so she said I should remember that in case something came up in the near future. As I was getting ready for work the next morning, I began putting my jewelry on. Every day, I wore earrings, bracelets on both arms, and a necklace I'd bought for myself several months before he passed. It was sterling silver, a thin chain with a double-overlapping heart pendant. One heart was plain silver and the other one sat slightly below it, outlined with cubic zirconia stones. I'd always preferred silver jewelry over gold and one day, I saw this necklace and thought it was pretty so I bought it for myself. Since I'd begun working at my new job, I'd received a multitude of compliments on that necklace. Over and over again, I was told by patients how pretty it was and how much they loved the double hearts. It wasn't just female patients either. There was even a male patient who remarked how much he liked it. He said he'd been looking for an anniversary gift for his wife and he really liked the double hearts.

Anyway, as I went to put my necklace on, I noticed the chain was broken. I stood there dumbfounded; how had this happened? I had taken it off and placed it on my bureau when I'd gotten home from the reading, the same way I'd done every other night for the past several months. How did it break? I looked closely to see if I could repair it but no, the eyelet had completely broken off of the chain and it wasn't a link chain so there was no way of attaching another one to it. It had snapped off so this chain was now useless. "Great," I said to myself. "Now, what am I going to wear?"

I decided to check my jewelry box for another chain I could put the heart pendant on. There was a similar chain in there, so I started to slide the double hearts onto it then paused and asked him, "What were you trying to tell me about hearts last night, baby? It was obviously very important to you and it can't be a coincidence that my chain mysteriously broke overnight. Now, I'm standing here holding these hearts in my hand. I know you're trying to get my attention about something involving hearts. I'll have to pay close attention from now on until I understand."

I put the pendant on the chain and wore it to work as usual. The compliments continued and I noticed each person made it a point to mention how beautiful the hearts were. It was never a general compliment about the necklace, but always a specific reference to the hearts. For whatever reason, that was the thing that always caught their eye and they felt compelled to let me know.

In the days following the reading, I thought a lot about the songs Tyger continued to send and what an amazing form of communication it had become. I was keeping a list and when I realized it was up to nine songs, I thought how great it would be to have them all in one place. I decided to purchase them and create a playlist on my iPod which I titled "From my Love." That way, I could listen to his messages of love one after the other anytime I wanted. What an incredible gift he'd given me through music. As I listen to the words, I'm assured they are coming straight from his heart to mine, things he wanted me to know and remember always. I felt his love, his admiration, and his gratitude for my love and I smiled. Even when the tears came, I found joy in these beautiful expressions of love. Whenever he chose to send a new message, I could add it to this playlist, put my headphones on, and escape the pain and loneliness without him. He made sure to mention this during the reading that I should "keep listening to the music." It still baffled me how I didn't understand the reference instantly, but then I was so overwhelmed by him being there, I should cut myself some slack. I knew he'd continue to communicate his feelings this way and he knew I'd be listening.

To this day, I wondered if that very first song he sent actually existed in this world. I'd never heard it in real life, yet I'd never forgotten the words or the melody. As many things as I forgot, for some reason, that song stayed etched in my memory which only convinced me more that it wasn't of this world.

These are the original nine songs he sent to me which I made into a playlist:

1.   *My Eyes Adored You (Frankie Valli & The Four Seasons)*

2.   *Outstanding (The Gap Band)*

3.   *Together Again (Janet Jackson)*

4.   *Guilty (Barbara Streisand & Barry Gibb)*

5.   *Every Woman in the World (Air Supply)*

6.   *Loving You (Minnie Ripperton)*

7.   *You are the Sunshine of my Life (Stevie Wonder)*

8.   *There's Nothing Better than Love (Luther Vandross & Gregory Hines)*

9.   *Caravan of Love (Isley Jasper Isley)*

Prior to the reading, my soul had already begun to awaken. I was convinced that there was more to life than what we could see, hear, taste, and feel in the physical world. Making contact with Tyger in the afterlife only confirmed that I had been correct. Along with this awakening came the empowerment to live according to my own certainties. Having said that, I was still unable to share the new truths I was now aware of. It wasn't out of fear of what people might think of me, because I had no need for anyone's approval of what I absolutely knew to be true. No, my caution about sharing my experience was a way of protecting myself from those who would use their own belief systems to try and discredit the connection between us.

Within my own family, there are many different faiths, several denominations of Christianity, and each group carried its own theories on death and what happened when we die. I had already been told so many different things by many well-meaning family members, ranging from, "He's sleeping and can't hear anything you say" to "Don't go to a psychic or a medium. Those are demonic spirits that come through to trick you."

In some ways, gaining this wonderful knowledge that Tyger was alive, always with me, able to hear me, still loving me, sending messages, and watching over me, isolated me even more. I was brought up to respect family, especially elders. How would I ever be able to tell them I did not accept what they were telling me? That I didn't have a single doubt in my mind that that Tyger was very much alive. At the same time, I knew there could come a day when I would have to say those things to people I respected and loved deeply. When all was said and done, I had to remain true to myself and maintain my self-respect. There was no way I could ever agree with someone telling me Tyger was sleeping or some evil spirit was pretending to be him. I knew at the deepest soul level those statements couldn't be further from the truth. For the time being, I knew it was best to keep this life-changing news close to my heart. It was my own private blessing, only to be shared with those who wouldn't crush my joy based on their belief system and/or personal fears.

My family was and has always been extremely important to me. The level of support I received after Tyger passed and continued to receive was a major part of the reason I was able to survive. My heart was eternally grateful and the love I had for my family was almost impossible to put into words. Yet, I was conflicted and saddened by not being able to share this incredible truth with them. More than once, I considered telling those I was closest to, the ones I had shared practically everything with for my entire life. I stopped short of doing that though as a form of self-preservation. I could not allow anyone - even people I'd trusted in the past with my deepest secrets - to rob me of this connection or to make me feel like I had to defend or justify what I knew to be true.

People had a way of telling you how they feel without uttering a single word. I would sense their disapproval and that would be just as bad, if not worse, than being told outright that I was wrong and this could not be happening. In order to maintain the relationships I held near and dear to my heart, I remained silent knowing all the while that should the subject ever come up, it could change things forever.

I would never deny his presence in my life or his continued love for me. If a day should come when that truth strained a relationship or two, then so be it. As Tyger used to tell me, "If the truth hurts, say ouch." This was one truth I would never doubt or deny... for anyone.

Following my contact with him, I felt such a lightness in my spirit. I spent quite a bit of time replaying what Tyger had shared with me during the reading and what a truly amazing experience it had been. After about a week or so it hit me: *There is no death.*

I had been so caught up in the happiness of our continuing connection that I hadn't paused to consider the bigger picture. The finality of death I'd always thought to be true wasn't accurate at all. The physical body does die, but that wasn't the real person. The body was merely a vessel that houses the spirit, the soul, the true *self.* The event known as death was really a transition from our physical form into the next phase of our journey. The fact that Tyger still existed with all of his memories from this life, as well as the ability to continue interacting with me, was all the evidence I needed. There was much more I wanted to learn, but I did know for sure the separation we associated with death was a grand illusion. Our loved ones were not lost to us and we remained connected by the love we shared.

My mother came through during my reading, as well. She expressed her love for me and also said I was a good girl, always a good girl. Laura explained she was holding rosary beads and instantly I understood why. I explained that I have my mom's rosary beads hanging on my bedroom mirror. I found them in her jewelry box after she passed. Here it was nineteen years later and my mom was still connected to me, aware of exactly what to say to prove it was her.

Death was the great lie that we've all been conditioned to equate with loss; the final ending. Instead, we should be viewing it as a doorway and a progression into a life beyond this one. There was no denying the pain we felt when someone we loved crossed over. The physical presence was suddenly gone, so we grieved and longed for the connection we shared. The devastation of having to live without physical contact with the man I loved was something I would endure until it was my time to transition. However, now that I knew he was alive and still with me, the light of hope shined in my heart alongside the pain.

During the reading, Tyger expressed so much concern for my financial well-being. That was one of the things that convinced me it was actually him speaking. He always made sure I had everything I needed in this life. He never wanted to see me struggle in any way. It made perfect sense he would speak about my finances. Since Tyger's passing, I'd had conversations with him on this subject, telling him I would be fine. I'd never been one who needed much, as long as the bills are paid and there was food in the house. That was enough for me.

As Laura relayed what he was saying: how much he loved me and his happiness with me She also said something I hadn't expected to hear which was Tyger's desire for me to find someone who could love and take care of me financially. Again, he said he loved me and knew how much I loved him. He also said I would always think of him; even in old age, I would remember him often. He didn't want me to go without and he wanted to see me happy. My initial reaction was, "Absolutely not. There's no way in hell I'm starting a new relationship." I expressed my reaction verbally as well, shaking my head and saying, "That's not happening." It bothered me that he had even suggested I do that until I had time to process the meaning behind it.

What an amazing expression of unselfish love that was. Even though he knew the depth of my love for him and our love for each other, he would put that aside to be sure I was financially stable in this life. How many people could say they were loved that deeply? I understood completely why he'd said that. It was right in line with the way he'd treated me throughout our relationship. There had been nights I'd planned to stop by and it would rain. He'd be so worried about me going out in the bad weather and we'd almost argue as I told him it was all right, I wouldn't melt and I was still coming. There were so many situations like that where he'd put my comfort first above his desires. He was doing the same thing, in this case, putting my comfort, my well-being above everything else. The fact he also said I would always think of him proved to me that he knew my heart was full of love for him.

As beautiful and unselfish as it was for him to say that, in the days that followed I explained to him it simply wasn't an option for me. I was as deeply in love with him as I was when he was physically here. My mind couldn't even fathom the thought of beginning a relationship with anyone else. I told him this was another one of those situations where he would have to let me have this one. Just like those times, he tried to get me to stay home because it was raining. I thanked him for loving me so much that he could put my well-being above everything else, but my heart didn't have the capacity to hold feelings for another man. The experiences and memories Tyger and I made together, the joy he brought and brings to my life fulfilled me in every way. His love sustained me and receiving validation he was still alive, that we would without a doubt see one another again took that love to greater heights. I reminded him of how his treatment of me during our time together had been a completely new experience. How I'd never known such happiness in any of the relationships I'd had before he entered my life.

I said to him, "Thank you, baby. I know why you said what you did, but my heart belongs to you. The money situation could be better, but it'll improve in time and I'll get there on my own. I long for you and only you and I know you're able to feel it. You see me every night smelling your shirt, your hat, your hairbrush. Every single night, I still do those things, trying to absorb your scent. You are my one and only, my everything. No one compares to you and our love."

I also told him there was no sense arguing about it.

"Remember the night you called and said you wanted to hang that shelf above your headboard, but didn't want to have to move the whole bed? I offered to do it since I could stand on the bed, but you kept saying no because it was almost nine o'clock and you didn't want me coming out late. I told you we could either spend the next twenty minutes arguing back and forth about it and I'd end up coming anyway, or I could just leave then and save us both some time. Well, this is just like that time. Enough said on that subject."

I laughed after saying that because I knew he would be amused by my closing argument. Both of us were stubborn by nature, but if I made a good case, he'd concede. This time, he had no choice. I had no way of seeing into the future or knowing where my journey would take me. All I knew for sure was at this stage in my life there was no room for a new relationship. There was no desire in my heart for anyone but Tyger, the man who improved every aspect of my life by simply loving me.

That weekend, Sophia and I went to the beach and she was gathering stones by the water. She ran over and said, "Look, Nani. I found a rock shaped like a heart."

Sure enough, it was a small, gray stone and it was heart-shaped. She used it to decorate a castle she was building.

The next day at the park she found a leaf that was also shaped like a heart. The following week, she found another heart-shaped leaf. I thought back to the reading and how Tyger kept showing Laura hearts. Sophia had drawn two hearts in the picture of him in the rain and then found that stone at the beach and the leaves. Maybe he was communicating with these hearts. These are messages he sends through Sophia. That made perfect sense to me and I continued to pay close attention to anything she said about him. She often shared random thoughts or would say things out of the blue about him.

One day, she said to me, "Nani, Mike protects us."

That was all she said and continued on with what she was doing. She knew how much he loved her in this life, so she would have no reason to fear him in any way. He loved her deeply and would never do or say anything to make her uncomfortable. I loved the connection between them and knowing that he watches over her. "His little baby" as he used to call her. She was his favorite little person and their bond remained intact.

A week or so after our contact, I was lying in bed early one morning. I was not quite awake, yet not fully asleep. I was on my back with my eyes closed when suddenly I felt someone poke me in my stomach. My eyes opened quickly and I expected to see one of my sons standing there. Even though this wasn't something either of them had ever done, I reasoned it had to be one of them. I was shocked to see no one there. I could still feel the sensation of having been poked in the stomach, but I was completely alone in my room. Right away, I knew it had to have been Tyger.

I laid there trying to process what had happened. This was physical contact and I was amazed. Even as I write about it, I can still remember exactly how it felt and how I was pulled out of my sleep. A true "wow moment" and even if it never happens again, it was unforgettable and very real.

I remembered the disappointment I felt early in my grief reading about the experiences of others who had received signs from loved ones. I often wondered why those things never happened to me. I questioned what was wrong with me and why wasn't Tyger coming through? What made those other people more worthy of getting messages than I was?

As I looked back, I realized the more open I was to receiving, the more I began to receive. The more I acknowledged his communications, the quicker he would send more. There was a time I felt it would never happen for me and I was destined to be sad and broken-hearted for the rest of my physical life. I clearly remembered how it felt, so I could relate to anyone who was desperate to hear from a loved one who had passed on.

My advice would be to have patience and never dismiss anything as being too small or insignificant. Signs are not always huge "wow moments." Sometimes they're quiet, subtle reminders that take your thoughts back to a place in time. Anything that feels as though it might be a sign probably is. Acknowledge it and be thankful. Ask for more and know you might not get a response right away.

Some of the messages that came through during the reading with Laura were things I'd wondered about after Tyger had passed away and hadn't thought about since then. He knew I still needed those answers, even though it had been a year since I'd asked the questions.

One of the best decisions I'd ever made was to contact that medium and have a private reading. When it was over I asked myself why I hadn't done it sooner. Instantly, I knew the answer was that everything happens in its time. It was the same with writing this book. After months of being told I should do it and even after receiving confirmation from my love, I still didn't start on it until it "felt right." This was a true labor of love and as I wrote, I tried to convey how deeply connected Tyger and I had become over the course of our continuing journey. How it progressed gradually and almost snuck up on us, in all honesty. When you entered a relationship with no real expectations and no demands except to just enjoy each moment as it came, anything was possible. Before we knew what was happening, we were each all the way in love with a person who had earned the other's respect. We admired qualities in one another and said what was on our minds. Neither of us had to guess what the other might be thinking or feeling because we shared what was in our hearts.

I wrote our story, being mindful of how I worded things. I needed the truth of our love to be clear in what I presented. There were days when I could write for hours and others when I don't write at all. I listened to my inner voice and to the guidance he gave me, as well.

One of the first decisions I made about this book was not to share publicly that I was writing it. The only person I told was Donna. I needed her objectivity and since she knew of Tyger's communications and never judged or discredited any of the wonderful things happening, I knew I could confide in her about my writing. Sometimes people could shoot down another person's dreams by invoking their own fears or insecurities on them. If I had made my work on this book common knowledge, there was a good possibility of that happening, even if it was unintentional. I decided to keep this to myself until it was in the publishing phase.

By keeping quiet about it also eliminated any pressure of being asked how it was coming or about the content. I could relax and let the words flow naturally, not according to anyone's suggestions or expectations.

This is *our story*, so it has to be told *our way* and in *our time.*

CHAPTER FIFTEEN
Love is Everlasting

AS I MADE MY WAY THROUGH this maze of grief, I spent quite a bit of time evaluating the process. One thing that came to mind was how after someone passed, they were sometimes made out to be some sort of saint. People tended to shy away from the dark days of that person's time in this life. That certainly wasn't my intention here. It was almost laughable to even think because the first person to tell you about Tyger's shortcomings would be Tyger himself.

As I said before, he owned up to the wrongs he'd done over the years and didn't make excuses for them. The same goes for me. I am in no way special or without my share of faults. I've done plenty in my life I'm not proud of and if I had the chance to do it over, there was much I would do differently. I've said and done things that hurt others over the years and for that I'm truly sorry. My purpose in telling our story is to simply share that we are two average people. Normal human beings who lived life the best way they knew how. We've loved, we've had our hearts broken, we've done good, we've done bad. We've been hurt and we've hurt others. We are no different from anyone else. We just happened to have been blessed with one another and through that blessing, we experienced the best versions of ourselves.

In a relatively short amount of time, we came to love each other deeply and formed an unbreakable bond. Our backgrounds couldn't have seemed more different, yet we shared our life experiences with each other and blended them into a deep understanding and acceptance. There were people who may have known him during his troubled times that still thought of him as the same person; someone to keep a distance from. That wasn't the real man, but that was what they knew of him.

The same was true for me, I was thought of as a true innocent in many ways. The quiet, shy, "good girl," yet I'd made choices in life that had caused others pain. When Tyger and I got together, we laid all of that right out on the table. No subject was off-limits with us. We talked about the things we'd gotten right in life and the things we'd gotten wrong.

We were two, regular, everyday people, whose lives had taken entirely different directions. Yet, somehow things were aligned in such a way that our paths crossed and we connected. The connection grew into a friendship which over time developed into the deepest love either of us had ever known. That love was the tie that bound us across time and space.

Realizing death hadn't robbed us of each other was a true gift. It restored my hope, my faith, and my very will to live. Never once did I ever imagine I would experience anything like this.

My point is if this is possible for us, it is possible for anyone. There aren't any magic words I can give you to establish this connection, it comes through love and believing it can happen and by being open and listening to that voice inside. The voice that constantly whispers to us, but we so rarely acknowledge. The more we trust the voice and the more open we become to the possibilities of what exists beyond the five senses. We've been conditioned to rely on those senses and deny the existence of more. By doing this, we are short-changing ourselves and limiting our experiences only to what is tangible.

I've lived the majority of my life doing exactly that, but now that my eyes have been opened to what lies beyond, there is no going back to the old way of thinking.

Even as I share these thoughts, I am very aware of the skeptics. I may have been one myself once upon a time. There are many who will say none of what I've experienced is real and they are certainly entitled to their own views and opinions. There is a quote I've read which says, "For those who believe, no proof is necessary. For those who don't believe, no proof is possible." Those words are absolutely true. Which is exactly why I choose not to debate this subject with those who don't believe.

My heart and soul know the only "death" is the shedding of the physical form. We continue on in a different place and remain connected to those we love. Our love remains current and active. Love is never to be used in the past tense when someone passes because it is constant and unbroken. Love is the only thing that truly belongs to us, the only thing we get to keep when we make our transition from this life into the next. Learning this great truth helps to put things into a clearer perspective. I've realized how little value there is in material things. We need them in this life and enjoy the comforts of our possessions, but they are all temporary.

As I continue to grow and learn more about our purpose in this physical part of our journey, I understand the importance of the relationships we build. Rather than being concerned with wealth or status, our focus should be on how we make others feel about themselves. That's the true measure of self, in my opinion.

To those who feel the messages delivered by a psychic or medium are the words of evil spirits, I couldn't disagree more. It is my understanding that something demonic or evil would want to draw one away from love. They would want to instill fear, hate, and darkness. Yet, my reaction to hearing these messages from my love on the other side have filled me with love and light. They have renewed my faith in an all-knowing, all-loving God. A God who designed life in such a way where we are allowed this communication. Love is the indestructible bridge that connects us. For me, it makes absolutely no sense whatsoever for these "evil spirits" to be delivering messages which bring me closer to God and love. Wouldn't that mean they were working against everything they supposedly stand for?

Again, I am not willing to debate this with those who feel it's the workings of the devil. To each his or her own. I can only speak for the effect on my life since learning the man I love is alive and always with me. It has opened my heart to a greater capacity for love than I've ever known. It has taught me the importance of showing love to others and spreading light whenever and wherever I can. My faith in God, our Creator, the

Higher Power, has never been stronger since having that reading. As I pray each night, it's with an even deeper belief that those prayers are heard and will be answered. Receiving proof life exists outside our physical form has drawn me closer to God and revealed how vast His love for us truly is. I am speaking solely from my personal experiences and the expansive way I now think of and view life.

Since my reading, I sometimes feel sorry for those who deny themselves the beauty of what I'm experiencing. There is no cure to stop the pain of missing our departed loved ones, but there is peace to be found in knowing how close they still are. That knowledge has changed my perspective on everything. Being reminded of how deeply Tyger loves me is empowering. My will to live has been magnified and I want to squeeze every ounce of enjoyment out of my days here.

What I mean by enjoyment is my intention of doing whatever brings me happiness from moment to moment. It may be found in a crowd of people or in the solitude of my own company. There are no set rules; I simply live according to what feels right. And, that is listening to the voice inside, my own intuition, and the whisperings of the man I love. Does this mean I live in a constant state of euphoria? Of course not. I have a new understanding of what it means to *live*. I refuse to spend my time worrying or full of fear. My focus is on putting my best foot forward and if something doesn't work out, then I'll lead with the opposite foot on my next try.

It's amazing how this outlook has reduced the stress in my life. I still have moments of agitation from time to time. I'm not immune to the frustrations that arise in day-to-day life. My attitude toward them is different now with those feelings being short-lived. The gratitude living in my heart is a constant reminder of "this too shall pass." Despite the longing I feel for Tyger's physical presence, it never overpowers the gratitude I feel for the love that connects us. Bitterness and negative emotions rob us of our true purpose in this life. We are here to learn how to love one another.

Following my contact with Tyger on the other side, I spent the majority of my time reflecting on what he spoke about. His message was clearly all about love: the love he feels for me and the happiness our love brings to him. Also, it was of his concerns for my well-being and his need to answer all of my questions. Every single part of his message pertained to love. The spirit of love in the air, while he came through to me, was so intense; it was like you could reach out and touch it. I felt wrapped up in it, engulfed by it, and surrounded by its warmth.

An observation I've made since then is as much as he loved his Cadillac and his many possessions, not once did any of that come up. There wasn't one reference in the entire reading pertaining to his "things" or what had become of them. For me, that was confirmation those items are only part of our physical experience. All of it is temporary and tied only to this life.

No matter how much we own or how much money we accumulate on this side of the veil, none of it matters on the other side. The one and only thing we own and can take with us is love. Despite the fact that Tyger is no longer in his physical body, he hasn't forgotten the way our love made him feel. The same is true for me. As thankful as I am for the many material things he gave to me which make my life more comfortable, none of them are as important as the way he made me feel and the impact his love had and continues to have on my life experience. In this life, we need our possessions in order to survive and bring us comfort. There certainly isn't anything wrong with owning things or having money. All I'm saying is we shouldn't place more value on our possessions than we do on our relationships. Those connections and the bonds we form with loved ones are what we get to keep when our physical journey ends.

When someone passes unexpectedly without a clear direction of what to do with their possessions, it's left for others to decide. It was no different when Tyger passed. There was speculation as to who should get what, as well as differences of opinion and suggestions on what should be done. Some pointed out what his final wishes were or what he would've wanted if he were still here. I began to realize how unimportant any of that was because it didn't matter to him now. Worrying about his "final wishes" or "what he would've wanted" was only being done by us *here*, not by him *there*. Coming to that realization allowed me to let go of those worries.

Whatever decisions were made about his material possessions no longer mattered. I would help however I could if anything needed to be moved or stored, but that was it. What had once belonged to him didn't make him who he was. They weren't the man whose love gave me the will to go on in this life. They were only objects, plain and simple.

Hearing the words he shared with me during the reading was confirmation of how little our possessions really mean when we leave this world. I have plenty of items around my house he gave to me and it brought so much joy to look at them. The beautiful memories helped to sustain me.

In this life, we crave the physical and tangible experience of touching what we own. I still enjoy this and one of my greatest pleasures continues to be my nightly routine of absorbing his aroma and handling his shirt, hat, and hairbrush. The memories rushed back to me every time I breathed deeply and inhaled his scent. The instant feeling of protection and safety that was triggered by the memory of being held tightly in his arms. I found joy in those possessions and the other comforts of my home. Those elements are a part of our "humanness."

After we shed our physical bodies, we leave our attachment to things behind. The only attachment that survives death is through the love that connects us. I spend my days looking for signs of Tyger. They turn up in unexpected places, but they are always there.

Each year, I go away with my aunt and cousins for what we call "Sista's Weekend." We book rooms in a hotel and spend time together, just us girls. No husbands or boyfriends or kids. Tyger loved the fact that I participated in these weekends, so I made the decision to attend in 2014, even though it had only been slightly over two months since his passing. He had known I was planning to go, so I felt it was important I attend. I did my best to enjoy myself, but during that time, the heaviness in my chest never left. Even if I appeared to be having fun, I was hurting and always aware he was missing.

The next year was quite different. I was able to enjoy every moment because I had been blessed with the knowledge that not only is Tyger still alive, he is with me always. The heaviness in my chest was no longer there. Even though I didn't feel comfortable sharing this truth with the others, it was wonderful having this private secret between Tyger and me. The weekend consisted of time in the Jacuzzi and the pool, going out to eat, shopping, and lots of laughter.

A group of us went to BJ's Wholesale Club and as we browsed around I tuned everyone and everything out and traveled back in my mind to the times Tyger and I had gone there together. As I strolled through the store, it was like I could feel him there, right beside me and my heart smiled. We also stopped at HomeGoods and although I was with my cousins, all I could think about was how much he enjoyed that store and our many trips there together.

At the end of one of the aisles, there was a display of clipboards for sale. They were made of clear plastic and the clip was gold. There was a white sheet of paper clipped to each one and printed on it in gold lettering were three words, "You got this." I stopped in my tracks, instantly remembering our days working at the casino. As a supervisor, I was required to wear a lab coat and I'd often carry a clipboard. Tyger had told me about a fantasy he had of me at his place, wearing nothing but my lab coat and carrying my clipboard. We had never actually done it, but we spoke about it several times and he had every intention of going through with it. When I saw those clipboards, in his favorite store, I recognized it instantly as a sign from him. I stood there lost in the moment reading the words attached.

"You got this."

I answered silently, "You're right, baby. I've got this."

Living and enjoying life is the way I can best honor Tyger. I know how much joy he feels when I laugh and smile. My goal each day is to continue being the woman he fell in love with. His "Over the top wow girl" as he used to call me. Being blessed with the knowledge that he still lives has given me permission to go on living. The changes happening inside of me are incredible and even though I'm experiencing all of it, I am in awe of the transformation.

At times, it feels as though my heart will explode with the happiness of knowing nothing is lost. I wish more than anything I could pass this feeling along to the rest of humanity; to those struggling with the terrible sting that comes with the death of a loved one. I know the sting so well; the feeling of utter despair, pain, and longing. The best I can do is to share our story and my experiences and offer hope to anyone who is suffering through the harshness of grief.

Even though we miss the physical presence of our loved ones, we can be assured we haven't lost them. We remain connected by the love we share and as long as we acknowledge that love, the connection is never lost. Hold on tight, don't let anyone cause you to doubt what your heart knows to be true. Stay open and receptive to love and it will always find its way in.

My outlook on life was completely and forever changed when I learned that death has no power over love. There is nothing and no one who could convince me of otherwise. Even knowing those things, I remain affected by the traumatic experience of Tyger's sudden passing. Moments of pain come unexpectedly and without warning.

In the fall of 2015, at the end of Daylight Savings, we turned the clocks back one hour. Nothing new about that; I'd experienced time changes every spring and fall for my entire life. This meant it would be dark by the end of my work day. It felt strange driving home in the dark even though I was leaving at the same time I always had since starting there. Each day I passed the hospital on my way to and from work, but up until this one particular day it had always been daylight.

As I approached the hospital on my way home, the sign at the entrance was lit. Seeing the hospital at night, in particular, the sign at the entrance, caused a sudden pain in my chest. That was the first time I'd seen the hospital after dark since the night Tyger passed and I was completely caught off guard by the emotions that came to the surface.

I had no idea something as simple as driving past the hospital after dark would have such an impact. For a split second, I flashed back to that night in my car, turning into the hospital entrance, not knowing his condition or what I would find when I got inside. I still carried hope in my heart even though I knew he was in serious condition. I was utterly devastated and completely heartbroken by his passing by the time I left.

A split second of driving the same route I'd driven for months to and from work had brought me back to the worst night of my life. This was all caused by the image of the hospital lit up after dark. I was unprepared for my reaction, yet the jolt in my chest was undeniable. Once again, my grief was manifesting itself physically. Although it didn't bring me to tears on this occasion, there was no mistaking how deeply rooted it still is within me. That brief experience was painful, but also a reminder of how far I'd come since the early days of my grief journey. I was aware of the heartache from that night, yet I was comforted by the knowledge Tyger was always near. It's difficult to explain how you can miss someone's physical presence so deeply while at the same time not feel alone. His spiritual presence and love are always surrounding me. The feeling is real and undeniable.

Since Tyger most often communicates through music, I pay close attention when a song seems to be stuck in my head for no apparent reason. This happened one day with Elton John's *Someone Saved my Life Tonight.* I woke up with the melody in my head and couldn't shake it. All morning, it was with me and I was humming along with it at my desk. It was such a beautiful song that I've always liked, but once again, it wasn't something I owned or had even heard recently. I pulled it up on the Internet and listened to the words.

Later that day, I searched online for the meaning behind the song. Apparently, many years ago, Elton John was planning to marry a girl which would've meant denying his true self. He supposedly attempted suicide and called off the wedding. The song is a testimony of his experience and he is speaking to his friend who saved him from a life of heartache.

I understood then why Tyger had wanted me to listen to that song. His message was I had saved his life by bringing so much love and happiness into it. In the process of saving him, he had saved me right back. His message to me during the reading had focused on our love and the happiness it brought to his life. What an amazing song to send; one I had to add to my playlist. I'm brought to tears when I listen to it:

"You're a butterfly and butterflies are free to fly, fly away... high away, bye bye."

Our love had given Tyger the freedom to fly high, to soar above any past hurts or bad experiences. Every ounce of that love is still with him, as it is with me.

I'm reminded of one of my favorite passages from the Bible, 1 Corinthians 13:4-7 (NIV) "Love is patient, love is kind. It does not envy, it does not boast, it is not proud. It does not dishonor others, it is not self-seeking, it is not easily angered, it keeps no record of wrongs. Love does not rejoice in evil but rejoices with the truth. It always protects, always trusts, always hopes, and always perseveres."

That is the most accurate description of love there is. To know I was blessed to have experienced love in its truest form during our time in this life is simply amazing. Add to that the affirmation I received from him on the other side, from his new life where all the pretenses of the human experience have been stripped away, and I am overwhelmed with gratitude. That's the reason I can say without a doubt that love is eternal and goes well beyond the physical journey. The phrase "power of love" takes on new meaning because there is no greater force in the universe.

As written in 1 Corinthians 13:13, "And now these three remain: faith, hope, and love. But the greatest of these is love."

Indeed, it is... it most certainly is.

CHAPTER SIXTEEN
The Journey Continues

EACH DAY PRESENTS NEW OPPORTUNITIES to be grateful. When Tyger passed away, I was overcome with immense pain and longing. However, even in my darkest moments, I never stopped thanking God for blessing us with one another. That was and is a constant practice in my life. Gaining the knowledge that he still lives and I haven't lost him has only magnified my level of gratitude. I approach everything I do with a positive outlook; always viewing the glass as "half full." That's not to say I don't miss his physical presence. Would I prefer to have him standing beside me to be able to reach out and touch him? Of course, I would. For the time being, though, I can accept that he *is* standing right beside me and he hears me when I speak to him. It's different now but I will see him again and my heart knows this time "apart" will seem like mere seconds. I embrace the opportunity to experience my purpose in this physical stage of my life. The lessons his love taught me in our time together helped prepare me for my present and future experiences.

There is no room in my world for negativity. I simply refuse to entertain it. The expression "misery loves company" is true. The complainers of the world seem to always be looking for someone to agree with them to justify their right to complain. Instead, I meet their negative words with positive alternatives. More often than not, they give up once they realize I can't be drawn into that energy. Spending my time appreciating the blessings in my life leaves no room for stress, fear, or worry. This peaceful existence doesn't mean I allow myself to be a doormat. In fact, the exact opposite is true. It gives me the confidence to stand up for myself because I've learned I have a right to protect my peace of mind. These types of interactions always come from a place of love; a love of *self* which is an essential part of life.

By keeping my thoughts positive and living with an attitude of gratitude, I'm more aware of the beauty in my surroundings. My mind isn't cluttered with doubts or fears and that allows me to be more receptive to communications from Tyger.

About a month after the reading, I woke up one morning and said to him, "Baby, I'm really missing you. I need a sign, something to remind me you're with me. Please, baby, send me something."

I went to work, expecting all day to hear from him in some way. It was a Friday, so when I got home, Sophia was there with Aaron for our weekend sleepover. She handed me a paper and said it was a surprise. I opened it and it was a drawing of Tyger and me. Two large hearts, side-by-side. In the first heart, she had drawn us holding hands. The second heart had two eyes and a huge smile.

I said to her, "Thank you, Soph. Nani loves it. You drew me and Mike holding hands and did such a great job. Why is the other heart smiling?"

She said, "That one means love and it's smiling because Mike makes your heart happy."

Her drawings had to be the sign I'd asked him for that morning, delivered by my granddaughter.

The following day, she and I went to the park. The weather was beautiful, nice October day, so we explored a trail which led to a bridge over a small pond. We stopped to look at the geese and talked about the pretty colors of the leaves on the trees. After the bridge, there was a gravel path leading into a wooded area. Walking along with my granddaughter, I was thinking of Tyger and how badly I wished he could be there with us. Just seconds after that thought, Sophia stooped down and drew a heart in the gravel. A few steps later, she drew another heart and recreated the drawing she had done for me on paper the day before. I looked up at the beautiful blue sky and mouthed a silent "thank you" to my love.

He'd heard my thoughts and was assuring me he was right there with his girls. He wanted me to know how close he always is and the strength of the connection between the three of us. What an amazing gift of love and devotion. I took pictures of her drawings on that gravel path, his messages of love, and proof he always hears me.

All at once, it hit me like a ton of bricks. He sent these hearts through Sophia as a sign he's always with us and always close.

Now I get it, baby. Now I understand what you were trying to show me during the reading.

How had I not seen this before? This little girl was always drawing hearts or finding heart-shaped things. The heart-shaped stone at the beach, the heart-shaped leaves at the park, the countless drawings on paper and then on the gravel path. Even that day in Tyger's brother's driveway, she drew hearts in the snow around the Caddy. He had been trying so hard to let me know he was right there, next to me, but I couldn't see past the sadness that was brought on from seeing his car again. Oh, my goodness, and my necklace. Compliment after compliment about those hearts. Constant reminders Tyger was so close and up until this point, I'd been completely oblivious to all of it.

As I replayed all of these occurrences in my mind, I wondered if he ever got irritated with me for not realizing it was all coming from him. This was like the night of the reading when he told me to *keep listening to the music* and I didn't understand what he was talking about until I was halfway home. I smiled to myself, picturing him shaking his head at it taking so long for me to finally get it. I imagined him saying, "Well, it's about time."

As I've said previously, the amazing revelation Tyger is still with me was something I kept mainly to myself. One of the few family members I felt comfortable sharing this news with was my goddaughter, Crystal. She and I have such similar views regarding spirituality so when she came back to Connecticut for a visit with her husband and son, I was thrilled to have some alone time with her. As I poured out the details of the reading and the undeniable proof I received of what happens at the end of physical life, she accepted every word with excitement. There was not an ounce of judgment or doubt in her eyes. Her reaction was both verbal and emotional and it felt so wonderful being able to share this news with someone so close to me. We spoke about how important it is to follow our own journeys in life and what a crucial role a positive attitude plays in our experiences.

She suggested I watch the movie, "The Secret." I'd never seen it, but I found it on Netflix and watched it later that night. I was completely blown away by what I heard. If anyone reading this has not seen the movie or read the book, I highly recommend it. They speak about The Law of Attraction and how the universe responds to the energy you put out. Living in a spirit of fear and doubt will continue to attract similar energy to you. Living with a positive attitude and feeling grateful for the things you already have will attract more positive energy and experiences to your life.

They go into much more detail in the movie, but as I watched, I said to myself, "Oh, my goodness. That's how I live my life."

For the most part, I've always had a positive outlook. There have been times, though, where I've allowed myself to become consumed by worry and/or fear. Since Tyger's passing, I'd experienced a complete shift in my thinking, first and foremost by being in a constant state of gratitude. Secondly, after coming through the darkest days of my grief, I began to gauge everything against that experience. Things others would have a meltdown over to me seemed like nothing after having survived such heartache. This allowed me to address the small things and immediately dismiss them. There was no holding onto residual negative energy because it served no purpose in my life.

As I learned more about the Law of Attraction, it became clear to me how I'd been able to find a job I loved so much. Way back when I decided to leave the casino, people would say, "Aren't you nervous about taking such a big chance? What if you can't find a job or can't get insurance?"

My response every time was simply, "I'll be fine."

I wasn't just saying it either I believed it. I never dreamt I'd suffer the unimaginable shock of Tyger's death so soon afterward, but even then, I never completely lost the feeling that I'd be fine.

My practice of praying before submitting each job application, thanking God for blessing me with the job and telling Him if I didn't get it, I'd know He had something better for me. That was sending a direct signal of gratitude and positive energy into the universe and causing things to shift in my favor. I was doing all of this without knowing anything about "The Secret" or the Law of Attraction. I'd never even heard of the book. Yet, I was a living testament to how true it was. Thanks to my gratitude and solid faith, I was blessed with a job that didn't feel like work to me. The quote, "Find a job you love and you'll never have to work a day in your life" applies perfectly.

I am as happy to go to work as I am to come home at night. At the end of my weekend, I have no feelings of dread for

Monday morning, no difficulty getting up when the alarm goes off because I look forward to going in each day. In my prayers every night, I thank God for my amazing job. Sometimes, I wonder if it bothers my co-workers that I'm always happy and bubbly in the morning, but that's how I feel and it lasts the entire day. I enjoy being there and it's obvious to everyone.

A patient asked me once if I enjoyed my job. When I answered yes, he said he could tell and I was definitely in the right line of work.

Now that I have an understanding of this law and how it works, it has opened my eyes to the things we often attract into our own lives. I am even more grateful for my positive outlook and the effect our relationship has had on my life experience. Tyger's deep, nurturing love for me healed past hurts and boosted my self-confidence. The pure happiness he and I brought to each other became a part of me. Even in my grief, the happiness he brought to my heart never left. The effect of our love created an abundance of gratitude and positive energy deep within me. Living in that state draws more of the same into my life, which, in turn, increases my gratitude and the cycle continues.

After my walk one day, I came home and started sorting laundry. I threw the clothes I'd been wearing in the washer and started doing housework. When I put that load in the dryer, I heard a noise that sounded like something metal rolling around inside. My heart sank when I realized it was my iPod. I'd left it in my pocket and had washed it by mistake.

Holding my breath, I tried to turn it on, but nothing happened. I was so upset because the iPod had been a birthday gift from Tyger. He'd given it to me years earlier and I loved it. How could I have been so careless? Why did I put it in my pocket? I always put it back in my purse after my walk. Why hadn't I done that this time?

I spent several minutes feeling sad, angry, and disappointed. Then, I said to myself, "Stop it. Put some rice in a baggie and put the iPod in there. If it absorbs the liquid and works again, great. If not, it's okay because you own the music and it's stored on your laptop so it's not lost."

I left the device in the rice for a few days, but it still wouldn't work. I accepted that, knowing one day I'll be able to buy myself another one and download my music onto it again. In the meantime, I could still play the songs on my computer or burn CDs to play on the stereo or in the car. Rather than focus on the loss in the situation, I turned my attention toward being grateful I still had the music. By doing that, I let go of the negative energy of disappointment and redirected it into something positive.

Every so often, I connect the iPod to the charger and attempt to turn it on. So far, it still hasn't worked, but I refuse to give up on it. Even if it never works again, I'll keep it forever. That iPod was one of the first gifts he ever gave me and I'll never, ever throw it away. Who knows? There may come a day when I press the power button and it comes on. I'm not ruling out the possibility, so it will stay right in the top drawer of my nightstand, next to his old cell phones I'll also keep forever.

Had I chosen to focus on what was lost, my entire day, week, month, could've been ruined. What purpose would that have served? I would've lost precious time that could've been spent enjoying life and, in the end, I still wouldn't have the iPod back. Dwelling on things we can't control is a waste.

Another example is the day I received notice of a certified letter waiting for me at the post office from the Department of Revenue. My initial reaction was fear.

"Oh no, what do the tax people want with me? This can't be good."

Instantly, I began running all sorts of negative scenarios through my mind. After a moment or two, I stopped myself, took a deep breath, and questioned why I was doing that. There was nothing I could do until the next morning since the post office was closed for the day. I had two choices: continue making up possible scenarios and ruin my night, or let it go, enjoy my evening, and find out what it was in the morning. Chances were it would be nothing and I'd have wasted a perfectly good night worrying.

I didn't give it another thought. I went on with my night as I normally would and when I woke up the next day it was without worry. I stopped at the post office on my way to the store and found out the notice was completely harmless. How upset would I have been if I'd wasted my time worrying all night and all morning, only to discover I had no reason to? I smiled to myself after opening that letter, knowing I had done the right thing by refusing to let it consume me. Through a simple shift in thinking, I was able to avoid unnecessary stress.

I am not immune to thoughts of fear and worry. My initial reaction in both situations was not a positive one. However, I was able to quickly shift my focus away from those negative emotions and concentrate on the bright side. I believe that's where most of us make our mistake, we get stuck in the worry or the disappointment and block our ability to see any hope. I can clearly remember times in my life when I'd been trapped in that cycle. Having experienced both types of reactions, I could honestly say finding the good in any situation was the best way to go.

I have to credit part of my ability to do this with having gone through the traumatic experience of Tyger's death. Grief is completely life-altering on every possible level. The most important lesson I've learned is the value of what's important and what isn't. Living life happy and stress-free is not only important, it's essential. Tyger taught me that in our time together in this life and continues to confirm it in his communications from the other side.

Tyger was a thinker. I used to tease him about how much time he spent thinking things out. Something he often said to me was, "The choices you make today will impact how you're living a month or two from now. I'm always thinking about how what I do now will affect me later."

Everything he did had been well thought out. He wasn't what you'd call a "fly by the seat of your pants" type of guy. One of his favorite analogies was the ripples formed by throwing a stone into a pond. Each ring represented a consequence of an initial action which is why it is so important to be aware of your actions. Part of living his life by design was to stay mindful of his goals and what he could do today to get him closer to them. As I learned more about the Law of Attraction, I realized Tyger had been living by these basic principles. His willingness to share his thoughts and ideas showed me the importance of focusing on what I want and how I can best get there. I have added this to the long list of lessons I learned from him, another reason to feel grateful.

When I speak about my gratitude for all the positives in my life, I imagine there are some who question my ability to do that. After all, the heartache of Tyger's passing surely can't be counted as a positive experience. On the face of that argument, those who feel that way would be right. Without a doubt, this has been the most painful experience of my life. However, his passing didn't happen *to* me or was a result of something I've done. It happened because he reached the end of his physical journey and made the transition into the next phase of life. Was I affected by it? Absolutely. I feel it in the very depths of my soul, yet I don't consider that a negative. The sorrowful emotions of that experience are a direct result of the love we share. Our love improved my life in every way imaginable during his time in this life. The happiness I experienced because of that love is something I wouldn't trade for anything. Even if I'd known in advance that events would play out the way they did, I would still choose our time together. His passing was literally a wake-up call to my soul. It opened my eyes to what lies beyond physical life and the eternal bond created by love.

By viewing things from this perspective, it's impossible to feel anything but gratitude. That doesn't mean I wouldn't give anything to have him with me physically, of course, I would. It just means I have a deep appreciation for the positive effect of our time together and the knowledge that we haven't lost our connection.

So often we attract circumstances into our lives without even realizing it. Following the accident with the deer, I was terrified of it happening again. Driving after dark became a nightmare for me as I was always expecting another deer to run out in front of my car. Since learning about the Law of Attraction and the power in our thoughts, I've made a conscious effort to eliminate those thoughts from my mind. By constantly worrying about what I didn't want to happen, I was sending a direct signal into the universe. The exact thing I was hoping to avoid is what I was attracting into my life by focusing so much energy on worrying about it. This has been one of the more difficult things for me to overcome but when I'm driving at night I reassure my mind that all is well, there is nothing to fear. I think about how grateful I am to have a reliable vehicle and how happy I'll be to arrive home safely. Always giving thanks for the positives and the many things I have to be grateful for.

My thought process is the same with my finances. I am so thankful as I pay each bill, even the times when there isn't anything extra left over. My focus is on how glad I am to have kept a roof over our heads, utilities on, gas in my car, and food on the table. Month after month, there is always enough money to cover the expenses and sometimes even a little extra. Even though on paper, I should be coming up short some months, that never happens. Somehow the universe finds a way to work it out and I continue being grateful.

Peace of mind is a priceless treasure. Before Tyger passed, I lived in a constant state of delight and harmony. After his passing, my existence was a one of torment and agony. Everything I'd ever known had been flipped upside-down and turned inside-out. There were days I couldn't imagine feeling anything other than sadness. The light of love and cheerfulness placed in my heart in our time together was never completely extinguished, though. It was dimmed by pain, but never went out.

As I found the path to healing, that light began to burn brighter and called to mind the bliss I'd once known so well. Over time, it became a balancing act between the sorrow of grief and the seeds of joy planted in my heart by our love. His beautiful signs and messages watered those seeds with hope and a promise of better days. I began to find my smile again and remember what it was like to laugh. Listening to him speak during the reading was the final step in happiness becoming dominate in my heart once again.

That was the day my peace of mind was returned to me. Once again, I recognized myself. I had changed in some ways, but I felt familiar, as though I'd been broken and was now reassembled. I wasn't exactly in the same order as I'd been before, but better, with more understanding and clarity of thought. I felt as though I had learned so much, yet craving even more knowledge.

The glimpse I was given into what lies beyond death has given me some idea of what it's like for him there. Far from a total understanding, but I was shown enough to know he's happy and still a part of my life. I can't even begin to imagine the beauty of where he is or what it's actually like for him, but I'm comforted to know he still exists in some form. I'd go for days, sometimes weeks, content with that knowledge.

All of a sudden, without warning, the tears fall from missing him. It catches me off guard but I don't try to suppress it. This happens sometimes at bedtime as I'm smelling his shirt. Every so often, his scent triggers a longing in my heart to see him, touch him, snuggle in close, and bury my face in his chest. No matter how enlightened I've become or how strongly I believe in the afterlife, nothing changes how deeply I miss him.

During those tearful moments, I lay in bed on my left side and imagine him laying behind me. With my eyes closed, I go back to the countless times I felt his body pressed up against my back and the safety I felt when he pulled me closer. The pure joy of simply being together..

For the rest of my time in this physical form, I will miss the contact. It doesn't take away from the gratitude of knowing he still lives or cast a shadow on the joy the knowledge brings me. Those two truths exist within me simultaneously, constantly running alongside each other. The sadness of missing him and the joy of knowing he's still with me. It's nearly impossible to understand and even more difficult to explain. I suppose it only makes sense to those who've experienced it themselves.

There is absolutely no time limit on grief. It took a tragedy of this magnitude for me to realize that. As I continue to post my feelings on my social media page more than a year since his passing, I know there are some who think I should "get over it already." To them, it seems like I'm dwelling and should be moving on. I forgive them because I once felt that way about others. Thinking to myself, "How long has it been? They still haven't gotten over it?" Of course, that was before my life was thrown into turmoil and ripped apart at the seams.

Grief is an ongoing, ever-changing experience. In the beginning, it was crippling, non-stop, physical pain. It hurt to do everything including something as natural as breathing. After the physical effects dissipated the emotional pain came to the forefront. My focus turned to missing our routine and suffering through the realization that all of it had just stopped. I despised the thought of going on in this life without him. As I began having contact with Tyger through signs and messages, it took the edge off of the pain and reassured me that some part of him still existed.

Now, I consider myself to be on the high-functioning side of grief. Finding enjoyment in life, feeling hope for the future and knowing without a doubt he is alive and well and always with me. Some would say my grief has ended, but that couldn't be further from the truth.

Quite honestly, I don't believe my grief will ever end. At least, not while I'm in this physical form. There will always be moments of sadness of wanting "us" back. Grief waxes and wanes, changes, and evolves. I can equate it to a vine growing along the side of a building. It twists itself around everything it comes in contact with, weaving in and out, conforming to the shape of what it encounters. That's how my grief behaves. It is intertwined with my life experiences, existing alongside my joyous memories. It has taught me to be gentle with others who are grieving and to let them know their grief is their own.

Knowing Tyger hears everything I say to him lets me know he understands what I'm going through. It shows me I don't have to worry about him mistaking my tears for doubt that he's still with me. He is aware of my feelings and what's in my heart. He remembers his human experiences and he knows the importance of physical contact on this side of the veil. The fact that he spoke about my appearance during the reading and the way he enjoyed me is proof he understands how difficult it is for me not being able to reach out and touch him. No matter what I'm doing, he is always somewhere in my thoughts. I function and go about my daily activities, but he is forever on my mind. It could be something that reminds me of him or a memory of a moment we shared. Sometimes it's knowing exactly how he'd react to something that's going on at the time. It makes no difference what the circumstances are I am always thinking of him. Even while I'm talking and laughing with friends, I'm still painfully aware of who's missing. He doesn't cross my mind occasionally, he stays there constantly.

Time has a funny way of moving on while simultaneously standing still. There are days I feel like it's been an eternity since I've seen my love and others when it seems like I passed him on the road yesterday. On other occasions, I can hardly believe I've survived this long without him physically here.

My understanding of the afterlife is that time has no meaning there. Everything seems to be happening all at once to those who've had near-death experiences. I told him one night, as I was speaking to our picture, "Maybe to you it feels like you just left here but it doesn't feel that way to me."

Moments of frustration find their way in at the thought of not making new memories together. That's one of the reasons I make it a point to be kind to myself as I move forward in my life journey. The word selfish is often given a negative connotation but it isn't always a bad thing. We need to dedicate a fair amount of time to ourselves, making sure our own needs are taken care of.

In moments of despair, I allow myself to feel those emotions so that I can move past them. It's much healthier, in my opinion, to let the feelings out, rather than suppress them and allow their manifestation to affect my physical health. In this life, we are in a constant state of learning. Some lessons are absorbed quickly and others take much longer. Grief has taught me how to be patient and how to empathize with others. It has forced me to take a good, hard look at myself in my most vulnerable state and decide between being a victim or a victor.

As my journey continues, I am proud of my accomplishments and grateful to have found my will to live again. Even during those times when the boundary between joy and pain becomes blurred, I never lose sight of my status as a victor. I remain the woman Tyger fell in love with, walking with her head held high even if I cried my heart out the night before. It makes no difference how big or small my steps are, the point is to take the next one and keep going.

CHAPTER SEVENTEEN
Unlocking the Power Within

SOPHIA'S ABILITY TO RECEIVE messages from Tyger is simply amazing. She passes them along innocently, having no idea of the incredible gifts she is giving to me. The love the two of them share for one another keeps them connected. I have to imagine it's much easier for him to communicate through her since her mind hasn't been corrupted by what is or isn't possible. At her age, everything is possible and there are no walls in place to block his messages. She simply listens to her thoughts without questioning where they came from and then shares them with me.

One day, she and I were in the kitchen making brownies and she asked, "Nani, what's your middle name?"

I answered, "Maria."

She said, "Oh, Maria Johnson?"

I said, "No, just Maria. Why did you say 'Johnson?'"

She answered, "I don't know."

I asked, "Whose name is Johnson? Do you know anyone with that name?"

She said, "No. I know a boy named John."

Sophia has known my first and last name since age three. I always had her practice saying it along with her Mom's and Dad's names and Markie's, in case anything should ever happen. There could only be one reason she would say the name "Johnson" without having any idea of why she'd said it. Tyger was right there with us. Johnson was his last name which was the reason I asked her whose name it was. I wondered if she knew this, but it was obvious by her answer she didn't. She also didn't quite understand why she'd even said it. The thought entered her mind and she repeated what she was thinking. She didn't question where it came from or even realize he'd whispered it to her.

The connection between the two of them is undeniable. The weekend after Thanksgiving, our town holds a Winterfest parade. Sophia and her mom were invited to be on the float of a local radio station in the 2014 parade, four months after Tyger passed. Sophia was so excited at the thought of being a part of it. Just as it was about to start, the float Santa was to ride on had a flat tire. They couldn't have the parade without Santa at the end. The radio station decided to give up their spot and let Santa use their float. This meant Sophia wouldn't be in the parade, after all.

Out of the blue, she was asked if she'd like to ride with Santa. Of course, she said yes. Not only was she in the parade, she was in the last float, sitting right next to Santa in his sleigh. This five-year-old girl had the best seat in the parade, smiling and waving to everyone as she rode through the streets at Santa's side. I wasn't there, but as soon as I heard what happened, I immediately recognized who had set things in motion. That whole scenario had Tyger written all over it. No way was his baby girl riding on some radio station's float. She had to sit right next to Santa, the main attraction, and the seat of honor, where everyone would be sure to see her. My heart was filled with joy at his unmistakable act of love.

The following year, she and I went to the Winterfest parade together. It was warmer than usual for November, temperatures were in the 50s but it was raining. I was undecided on whether or not to go because of the weather. It wasn't pouring, so I figured we'd be okay with our umbrellas. We would walk downtown since I live so close. There was no sense in doing anything with my hair in the rain, so I threw on a baseball cap. Sophia asked where her pink hat was since I was wearing one, she wanted to also. Tyger had bought her a pink New York Yankees cap, with a pink cupcake on the visor and that's the hat she wanted to wear. We put our hats on, grabbed our umbrellas and chairs and set out for downtown.

We were enjoying the parade, clapping and waving to the people as they went by. There was a woman next to us taking pictures of each group as they passed. She turned and asked if she could snap a photo of Sophia.

"She is so adorable in her pink hat with that pink umbrella. Do you mind if I take her picture?"

"No, I don't mind" I answered. "Go right ahead."

When the parade ended, we walked back home, changed into some dry clothes, and snuggled up with blankets to shake off the chill from being out in the rain.

A couple hours later, her mom sent a picture of Sophia to my phone. It was the photo the woman had taken of her at the parade. I was confused. Did this woman know Sophia's mother? Had she sent the picture to her? A few seconds later, her mother sent a text saying the picture was posted on the parade's Facebook page. I couldn't believe it. That woman had been taking pictures for the official page of the Winterfest parade and chose to post a picture of my granddaughter. Not only that, but she specifically mentioned how cute she looked in her "pink hat" the one Tyger had given her. Without a doubt, this was orchestrated by him. It was a sign to let me know he was with us and, once again, he wanted her involved in the parade. Such an amazing feeling came over me, the warmest feeling of love. I smiled and spoke to his picture.

"You are something else, you know that? You sure do know how to get my attention. Thank you, baby. Thank you."

The powerful connection between them is what allows him to deliver so many messages through her. These messages are so strong and clear, they actually stop me in my tracks.

What I wouldn't give to have the innocence of a child. For my mind to be a blank slate, able to receive information without the corruption of what society has set as the standard. Although I was good at recognizing the signs he sent, both through Soph and directly to me, I wanted to be better. I also recognized the importance of acknowledging every one of them and thanking him each time. Yet, I knew my ability to communicate with my love needed to be fine-tuned.

Our connection had been confirmed during the reading; he made it a point to let me know I was right about the signs he was sending. However, I wanted to learn how to be open to his messages. How could I reduce the noise of life on this side to allow me to hear him more clearly? As thankful as I was for all the communications from him, I always longed for more. During the quiet periods between messages, those pesky feelings of doubt would creep in causing me to wonder if he was with me all the time. It angered me when my faith wavered, yet it was something I couldn't control. Those doubts never stopped me from speaking to him or believing he could hear me, but I would ask for more and new signs to show he was close. When those signs didn't show up right away, that's when the doubt crept in.

When the holiday season approached in 2015, it marked the second one I would face without Tyger physically here.

Was it easier?

Well, yes and no.

I was grateful the heaviness in my chest wasn't constant, but at the same time, I was saddened by the fact that time continues marching on without him. I had no idea of how I would afford Christmas since I was barely able to cover my monthly bills. Add to that the fact I needed snow tires for my car and soon would have to purchase heating oil for the house and you can understand why I was feeling some pressure. As much as I love my job, the pay is significantly less than it was in my former career. That's fine with me because it's impossible to put a price tag on the peace of mind my new career has brought to my life. Still, less money coming in made it difficult to make ends meet.

I was happy to learn I qualified for the annual bonus being given out, although I had no idea how much it would be. I hoped and prayed it would be enough to pay for my snow tires; being December in New England time was of the essence. Thankfully, it had been a mild month with no snow in the immediate forecast but January could very well be a different story.

The plan was to get snow tires with the bonus check (hopefully), then buy Christmas gifts for my sons and grandchildren out of my regular pay. I wouldn't be able to get them anything big, but I knew they wouldn't mind. My need to buy gifts was more about me than it was about them. They've never known a Christmas without something under the tree and I certainly didn't want that this year.

When I received the bonus, it was significantly less than I'd hoped for. I was so grateful to receive anything, but it didn't come close to covering the cost of tires. That meant there was next to nothing left for Christmas shopping including the extra food for our holiday dinner. My heart sank when I saw the amount of the check. I couldn't help but be torn between gratitude for getting it and disappointment it wasn't more. I sat down and calculated what I'd need for the bills, tires, etc., and felt sick about not being able to afford Christmas.

My feelings weren't brought on because my sons were expecting or demanding anything from me. They knew my situation and totally understood. I'm fully aware Christmas isn't about the gifts, but even knowing that, the thought of not being able to give them and my grandchildren, at least, a little something was breaking my heart.

I recalled how it had been when Tyger was here, how he always wanted to contribute toward Christmas. A few years earlier, I had finished all my shopping and had all the gifts wrapped and under the tree.

He handed me some money and said, "Go to the store and buy Soph a bunch of toys. Nothing big or expensive, just a lot of little things you can wrap and put under the tree. I want the presents overflowing when she wakes up Christmas morning."

I did as he asked and her eyes lit up when she all those gifts. He was always so giving, so willing to take care of everything.

My lack of resources was heartbreaking and when I went to bed that night I spoke to him about it. Telling him how I didn't know how I would pull it off this year. I began my prayers in the same way I'd done every night, thanking God for blessing Tyger and me with each other. Thanking Him for my loving sons, my healthy grandchildren, a job I love, my reliable vehicle, and all the other blessings in my life. I expressed my gratitude and explained my sorrow for what I was feeling. I sighed as I said goodnight to my love and then turned off the light to drift off to sleep.

I began to dream of Tyger and me. We were riding on a bus, seated across from each other and we were talking about his brothers. We were discussing how different their personalities were and I kept telling him to lower his voice because one of them was sitting toward the back of the bus and I didn't want him to hear us. He was laughing in his usual way, which was also making me do the same. I was enjoying it so much, oh, how I'd missed that.

All of a sudden, I woke up and I faced the alarm clock by the bed. It was right after 5:00 a.m. and still somewhat dark in the room. I looked away from the clock and there standing directly beside my bed was Tyger.

I blinked several times and each time I did I could still see him standing there. He was less than a foot away from me, towering over the bed. He had his black baseball cap on and a dark blue windbreaker with white stripes down the sleeves; a jacket he'd worn often. His size was exactly right, my big strong man standing there at six-foot-five with those big, broad shoulders and his hat turned slightly to the side. I was utterly in shock and couldn't speak a word.

All I kept thinking was, *"This is real. This is real. Oh, my God. This is really real."*

I stared for a second at his full silhouette. He didn't appear to be transparent in any way, but I felt almost paralyzed like I couldn't reach out and touch him. He started to lean in as though he was going to whisper something to me or maybe kiss my face. I closed my eyes for another second and when I opened them he was gone.

I laid there assuring myself this had really happened and then fell back to sleep. I woke up when the alarm went off and instantly recalled him being there. I remembered the dream and our conversation on the bus and then how I'd woken up to see him standing right by my bed. It was as though he was watching over me as I slept.

I recognized this visit as his way of assuring me all would be well. He was with me as he always had been and I had nothing to worry about. I spoke to his picture, thanking him over and over for the visit and such a beautiful message. Nothing could bring me more comfort than seeing him and knowing how close he always is.

As I got ready for work, all I could think about was seeing him standing there, right beside my bed. He was close enough for me to touch, although I hadn't tried to. I wondered what would've happened if I had.

Damn it, Diane, why didn't you try?

It was the strangest thing to be awake and know I was awake, but unable to move. I thought back to the morning weeks before when I'd felt him poke my stomach. Had that been his first attempt at coming through physically? I wondered how many times he'd tried before actually being able to do it.

I thought about the movie *Ghost* when Patrick Swayze's character was getting frustrated trying to learn how to connect with Demi Moore's character. I realize it was only a movie, but compared to what I was experiencing, it seemed like a good point of reference. I also remembered how after Tyger passed, I would purposely walk around my house at night in the dark, praying I'd see his silhouette standing there. I would sit up in bed in total darkness, calling out to him, hoping to see his outline in a corner of the room. After several nights of doing that, I finally gave up. Now, here it was over a year later and he did it. He actually did it and I was thrilled.

I couldn't wait to get to work and tell Donna all about his visit. She was as overjoyed as I was and reacted with excitement. I explained how sure I was that he was really standing there and how I could clearly see his size and shape; recognizing the clothes he wore. His appearance was right in line with other accounts I'd read of people who've been visited by loved ones on the other side. They always seem to be dressed in familiar clothes, the same way they'd dressed in this life. I told her how comforting it was to see him, not frightening in any way. It had been more than a year since I'd laid eyes on him in person, but everything was how I'd remembered and exactly as it should be. Seeing him there felt like returning home after a long trip. It seemed perfectly comfortable, familiar, and *right.*

Donna and I spent the morning talking and marveling at how incredible my experience had been. Before we knew it, it was time to start our lunch breaks.

When I returned from lunch, Donna pointed out a lady in the waiting room who had come in asking for me. She was told I was at lunch so she said she'd wait until I got back. I looked out and recognized her as a person who'd come into the office for an appointment the day before. She had come to my window to be checked in and I realized she and I had gone to high school together.

I greeted her and said, "I remember you from high school. My name is Diane Santos. How have you been?"

She looked at me for a minute and then said, "Yes, I remember. How are you? Has life been good to you?"

I answered, "Yes, I have two sons and three grandchildren."

I showed her Sophia's picture and asked how life had been for her.

She said, "It's been good. I recently lost someone close to me."

I told her I was sorry to hear that and said, "I also lost someone. Just over a year ago, I lost the love of my life."

I pointed to a picture of Tyger and I and she said, "Oh, I'm so sorry to hear that. It must be so hard for you but still you look great."

She asked his name and if he had gone to school with us. I told her his name was Mike Johnson and he was older than us. I thanked her for her sympathy and noticed she seemed to be deeply touched by what I'd shared with her. We said a few more words and then she took a seat in the waiting room. She was there for a monitor which she would have to return the next day. So, that explained why she was back again, but why would she be waiting to see me?

I walked out to the waiting room to say hello and she asked if I could sit for a moment. She began telling me how moved she had been by what I'd told her the day before about losing the love of my life and how it had stayed with her for the rest of the day. She explained she's an empath and when I told her about Tyger, she picked up on our love right away. When she woke up the following morning, she heard music playing in her head and thought to herself how beautiful it was. After a few seconds, she realized it was *Send One Your Love* by Stevie Wonder. The song was followed by a message from Tyger. He was holding out a bouquet of roses which were meant for me. As she told me this, she picked up a bouquet of a dozen red roses that were on the chair next to her and handed them to me.

She said, "These are for you from Mike. He also wants you to have this."

She gave me a piece of paper rolled up and tied with a small red ribbon. She had written on the outside, "Hello from the other side."

When I opened the paper, it was the lyrics to the beautiful song he'd sent, his message of love to me:

Send her your love, with a dozen roses, make sure that she knows it, with a flower from your heart.

While reading the words, the tears poured from my eyes. I looked up at her and told her he had appeared to me early that morning. For the first time since his passing, he had actually appeared beside my bed and now here she was delivering this message out of the blue, just hours later.

She explained she had hesitated to do it because she didn't know if I'd think she was crazy showing up at my job with flowers. Tyger was very insistent and her spirit guides were pushing her so she had to listen.

I cried and hugged this woman, a virtual stranger to me who I hadn't seen in thirty years. Yet, here we were connected in such a profound way. She told me not to doubt I'd actually seen him that morning. His spiritual strength allowed him to come through so I could see him. This was further proof of how powerful our connection was to one another. We laughed at how busy he'd been in the early morning hours, appearing in my room and communicating to her what he needed me to see and hear.

The message he wanted her to pass along to me was there is no separation. We are always together; we always have been and always will be. We are true soul mates and we share one heart. She told me how strong the love is between us and how deeply connected we are to one another. She described him as a powerful spirit, strong and determined to get this message to me.

In addition to his strength, she said the light shining from within me is as strong and powerful as his. He asked her to tell me he and I entered into a soul contract long ago and there is something extremely important the two of us are supposed to do together. She didn't know what it was, but she said whatever it is it would have a huge impact on others.

When she told me this, I immediately thought of this book. It is the telling of our story which is something he and I have been writing together since the beginning. I've been receiving his messages which validated everything I'd been experiencing. I felt renewed and alive again, just as I'd felt after his messages at my reading with Laura.

Somehow I managed to get through the rest of the afternoon at work, staring with love and disbelief at the beautiful red roses on my desk. This was one of the biggest *wow* moments yet. He actually found a way to send me roses and if anyone could do it, he could. When I got in my car that evening, I found the song on my phone and cried all the way home listening to the beautiful words:

I know people say two hearts beating as one is unreal, and can only happen in make-believe stories. But so blind they all must be that they cannot believe what they see, for all around us are miracles of love's glory.

My man, my beautiful, romantic, real man had found a way to once again touch the depths of my soul to silence the doubt, the fear, the worry, the stress, and remind me that all is well because we have each other. All the money and jewels in the world couldn't buy the peace it brings to my spirit.

Another beautiful song to add to the playlist from my love. When I purchased it, I thought about moving it to the number one spot, but decided to keep the songs in the order he'd sent them. Since my iPod was no longer an option, I burned two CDs - one for the car and one for the house - so I wouldn't have to carry one back and forth whenever I wanted to listen to our songs. I feel so comforted when I hear the music he's sent to me. It's like having a direct line to him. I believe he's right there listening with me. The beautiful words express so much and tell exactly what he wants me to know. It's such an amazing way of communicating and quite often a verse will speak directly to my heart, bringing me to tears. These are not from sadness, they come from my deep appreciation of his love and the bond we share.

There is no reason for me to ever feel lonely because we are never apart. The connection is always there and he had to grab me and shake me to open my eyes to it. The messenger he chose to do this couldn't have come from a more unlikely source. A girl I went to high school with and someone who I knew of but never associated with. We had a completely different circle of friends, but I knew her name and we may have shared a class or two. When she came into the office that first day, I almost hadn't mentioned that I'd recognized her. A voice inside prompted me to tell her we had gone to school together which set things in motion for what would become a mind-blowing experience for both her and me. She had no way of knowing how I'd react to her showing up with flowers and this fantastic story. What a huge leap of faith she took by even going through with it. There is no possible way I could ever begin to thank her enough for having the courage and compassion to deliver his message to me. I hugged her and told her I would be eternally grateful for her being brave enough to take that chance. Surprisingly, she thanked me, as well, for sharing our story and the honor of conveying Tyger's message of love.

I was able to enjoy Christmas with my sons and grandchildren. Tyger had come to reassure me all would be well and he was right. There were presents under the tree for everyone and although I wasn't able to do as much as in past years, everything was given with love. We were together as a family and his presence was felt. As I watched my family open their gifts, I was filled with gratitude for his influence on my life. His ability to somehow make everything all right, to always let me know there's no need to worry. If he could find a way to appear in my room and send me flowers, how hard could it be for me to afford a few gifts? That became my mindset and the anxiety I'd felt melted away. I was able to relax and let things happen.

Once again, the universe had aligned things to play out exactly as they were supposed to and the end result was nothing short of a miracle. It is my understanding we all have some amount of psychic ability. For most of us, it manifests in the form of a gut feeling or as something we seem to know instinctively. I'm certainly not labeling myself as a psychic, but I do recognize the connection between Tyger's soul and my own, as well as the connection between him and Sophia. Communicating in this new way requires patience and faith, but there is no denying it when it happens. All that time I'd spent longing for a deeper connection to him, little did I know it had always been there. This secret ability I'd been unaware of had simply been locked away, waiting to be recognized.

Now that I've acknowledged and embraced this truth, there are no limits to what's possible between our souls. One of my most amazing discoveries has been learning that the power I'd been searching for has been mine all along. All I had to do was look within myself to find it.

CHAPTER EIGHTEEN
Always Hello

THERE IS NO END TO LOVE. I have absolute, undeniable proof of that.

In the beginning, all I could think about was how I'd lost Tyger and how he was gone from my life forever. Nothing could've been further from the truth. My world is so full of him, of *us*, that losing him is impossible. Add to that the proof he still lives and is always with me and I can say with confidence that love is eternal.

I'm not pretending to have all the answers, nor do I claim to have everything figured out about the afterlife. There is much I don't know and I'm eager to continue learning. Even with my limited insight, I'm aware of enough to be certain we are eternal beings. I believe we are only exposed to as much as we consider to be possible. As we expand our view to the potential of what exists beyond the physical experience, more is revealed to us.

Every single one of us is at a different stage in their journey. For me to try to force my truth on someone who isn't ready would be pointless. In turn, for someone to try and discredit what I've already had proven as absolute fact would be ineffective. In my opinion, this is where religion falls short. The emphasis is often on justifying one faith while disproving that of another group. If only more of us could live in a state of acceptance, tolerance, respect, and love. Forget the subtle differences in belief systems and simply love one another. To speak of condemnation for not following certain doctrines only invokes negative energy.

I go through each day with the knowledge that I will see Tyger again. Would I prefer to have that happen sooner rather than later? Without a doubt. Since I don't have a say in when it will happen, though, all I can do is go on living. Wallowing in sadness and despair won't do anything but attract more of the same. I am incredibly thankful for the undeniable proof I've received that he still exists. It has been the true catalyst in my renewed will to live life as fully as I can. To dream big and reach for things I'd never before imagined possible.

In my prayers and as I write this book, I continuously ask for my words and experiences to touch the hearts of those who need hope. My deepest desire is to help others who are suffering from the trauma that comes with the death of a loved one. I would not wish this on anyone, yet it's a hardship we are all confronted with at some point.

I hold no degrees on the subject, I haven't studied grief counseling techniques, and I certainly don't claim to be an authority on this. What I am is someone who is living it. An ordinary person who was blind-sided by unimaginable heartache. I navigate through the darkness by holding on to our love and my faith in a Higher Power.

I am still told of my strength, but people only see what I allow them to. The pain in my heart is as much a part of me as an arm or a leg or any other body part. Sometimes it lies dormant for a while and then out of nowhere it's back without warning. All of a sudden I'm made aware of how real and agonizing it is to be here without him physically. In the middle of my tears, sometimes a burst of anger surges through.

"Why did he have to go? I miss *us,* I want *us* back."

Regardless of how much time has passed, our routines are still fresh in my mind. I often have to think my way out of the anxiety that comes to the surface. The gripping fear at the thought of never experiencing any of that again in *this life.* As sure as I am of an afterlife and with all I've heard about how wonderful it is, the fact remains the only existence I can relate to right now is this physical one. I grieve for the loss of that part of our journey together which explains why there is no end to the sorrow, at least not while I'm still here.

I hold on tight to the happy memories we made together. Sometimes, I try to picture how it will feel when we see each other again and realize the suffering is over. Just the thought of seeing Tyger's smile causes my heart to race with excitement. I'm aware that each day I spend here missing him brings me one-day closer to our reunion. That knowledge uplifts me and fuels my will to go on. He was clear in his message during the reading that right now it's my time to be here. So, I accept that and try to focus on how much of him is still with me. I think of the places we visited, the rides we took, the laughs we shared, the love we made... all those things are mine to keep. The feeling of being cherished and protected continues to surround me. The pure adoration in his eyes when he looked at me is a beautiful memory. The intensity of our incredible bond has not been diminished in any way.

Of all the many things I'm grateful for, I'm extremely thankful his passing didn't fill me with bitterness. Those early days were indescribably difficult and the pain was far beyond anything I'd ever experienced. Yet, somehow, by the grace of God, I was able to hold on to the joy we'd brought to each other's lives. Even when I wasn't aware of it, I was hanging on by a thread. That thread became a string, then a rope, and eventually the life line I used to pull myself back into the world. My heart knows he will always guide and support me in all I do. Lifting my spirits and sending messages to confirm our connection.

I fell in love with a man who was larger than life. Someone who preferred privacy and followed his own set of rules yet touched so many people. In his time here, I don't think he realized the impact his friendship had on others, but I hope he is aware of it now. During the reading, Laura spoke of his strength in spirit, how he was coming through so clearly and had so much to say. When my former classmate delivered the roses and his message, she told about his powerful energy. Those descriptions were, even more, confirmation that this really was him because he had such a commanding presence in his time here, as well. My man found a way to send me a dozen roses from the afterlife. How spectacular is that? The magnitude of the gesture is further proof to my heart that he still lives. He loved to do things that were "over the top" and sending those flowers certainly falls into that category. They symbolized our ongoing relationship, and I marveled at how incredible love is. My heart once again assured there is nothing that can break the bond of true love.

I have to imagine it's difficult for those who have passed on to communicate with us in the physical world. What I mean is they have to compete with a multitude of distractions. It must require a fair amount of patience and perseverance on their part to keep trying to get through when so few are truly ready to receive. Even those of us who are open to it can miss things during the moments we're consumed by our grief or engrossed in everyday activities. It's not always easy to slow ourselves down enough to actually listen, but it's so important that we do.

For those who don't believe in spiritual connections or can't see beyond the tangible, I sincerely hope one day they will be able to. They are missing out on so much by remaining closed to even the possibility. The fact is, though, their incarnation is on a different course than my own. I'm not trying to convert anyone, although if I can help to expand someone's view, then that's wonderful. My desire is to tell the story of my love and me and the facts of our connection, both before and since his passing.

Early in my grief I desperately needed to hear of hope, to read the accounts of others that were close to what I was going through. To me, it would be selfish *not* to share our story; to keep these extraordinary, wondrous events from reaching those seeking validation of their own experiences. In the very least, I pray this will shed light on what's available to all of us if we can have faith and believe. Even the slightest shift in thinking from "impossible" to "maybe" begins to remove limitations, allowing signs and messages to come through. It definitely takes some getting used to and can be difficult at times, navigating this new way of exchanging information. I can't tell you how often I've said to him out loud, "I wish you could just pick up the damn phone and call me." It does become easier, especially when you acknowledge their efforts and stay grateful always.

As you become more awakened, don't be discouraged by those who are not ready to hear about your connection with the other side. Even the most well-meaning family and friends can crush your hope with their reactions to your messages from loved ones passed. I understand the disappointment of not being able to share certain things with those closest to us. Rather than get upset with them, disclose only what you feel comfortable with and pray for their enlightenment. I find it's much easier on my spirit to take this approach, rather than try and force my reality on those who aren't prepared to receive what I already know to be true.

There are some who may simply refuse to accept any of what you're experiencing. I know full well for every magnificent sign my love has sent me, there is someone out there with a "logical explanation" of how it may have happened. Those are the ones I pray for. First, that they never have to know the excruciating, debilitating pain of having a loved one ripped from their lives. Second, that somehow the light of truth will enter their hearts. The first step to opening the mind has to come from changing the heart. Oh, the wonderful revelations that will be available to them if they can only begin to wake up.

Remember always to be gentle with yourself. Some days you'll feel like you and others you won't recognize a single thing about your life. Cry when you want to, scream when you need to, smile with the happy memories and take each moment as it comes. There is no right or wrong way to survive grief. Every one of us will handle it in our own way and our own time.

The last thing I wanted to hear about was stages or how I should or shouldn't be feeling. My emotions are processed on a moment-to-moment basis, focusing on what's best for me. The only person I'm concerned with impressing now is myself. By nature, I've always been somewhat of a loner, but this life-altering experience has reiterated the importance of taking care of me first. Failure to make my well-being a priority would render me incapable of helping anyone else. It's impossible to pour from an empty cup, so we have to replenish ourselves regularly or we have nothing to give. Whether it be love, compassion, advice or anything else, it begins with self-love.

For a long while, I thought I'd never have a reason to laugh again. One day, I caught myself giggling about something the two of us had found amusing and it felt good to do that. It came with sadness, too, missing our fun times together, but it was a step toward healing. Releasing emotions in a positive way instead of constant tears was sorely needed. Listening to his words being relayed by the medium reminded me of why I'd fallen in love so deeply with this beautiful heart. That charisma, that warm, loving, funny personality and "no bullshit" attitude had drawn me to him. Every one of those qualities was what made him who he was and still is.

We've been conditioned to picture those in the afterlife as these chubby angels who can do no wrong, flying around with their wings and halos, but now I know that's not how it is. The core of who we are remains the same. The best parts of us stay with us and he is still the marvelous soul I know and love. The ego and prideful feelings are human qualities that die with the body, but we keep our basic personalities. Everything I love about Tyger is still in him.

Speak to your loved one and don't be afraid to ask for signs. They will hear you and respond. Be patient and pay close attention to what goes on around you. Sometimes their answers come in unexpected ways.

Several weeks before finishing this book, I asked Tyger for his help. I wanted to know if I had included everything that needed to be told. I was worried about the ending, in particular, and had come to a stand-still with my writing. Walking alone at the park, I spoke to him out loud.

"I need your help, baby. Can you find a way to tell me if there's anything else I should write about that I haven't touched on already? Our story is so beautiful, so real. After all our 'wow moments,' I don't want this book to fizzle out at the end. I want to finish strong so we can share our gift of love with the world. I really don't know what to do, so I need you to show me somehow. Please send a message and tell me if there's something else we have to say. No one I know is able to get things done the way you are, so let's do this together."

That was it.

I asked for his help and I waited for his response.

In the days that followed, I continued speaking to him as I always do, about everyday things and, of course, my usual talk with him at bedtime. Even though his answer didn't come instantly, I never doubted he'd heard me and would find a way to let me know.

He acknowledged my plea in a way I never would've imagined he would by somehow manifesting himself beside my bed while simultaneously putting the second half of his plan in motion. His answer came through loud and clear with a bold exclamation point at the end. I asked him to help us finish strong and that's exactly what he did. Never in a million years would I have envisioned him standing in my room in what I'd consider physical form. Not once, since I began writing our story, did I expect to witness such an amazing feat. That alone wasn't enough for Tyger though. His pretty baby asked for help, for another "wow moment," so he sent a beautiful song with roses and a detailed message. He didn't respond with an obscure sign or vague symbol. He had a living, breathing person relay his thoughts and love verbally so nothing had to be left open to interpretation. He also made sure this happened at my job, with people around to witness it.

His words of love were clear and concise:

We are true soul mates. We have always been together and we always will be. There is no separation. We set out to do something very important together that will have a huge impact on others. Our love is our strength and what connects us. We share one heart and I am always with you.

As I continue to grow and move forward in my journey, it is with absolute certainty that he walks beside me always. No matter what I may be faced with during my remaining time here, I will never be alone. There will be occasional sadness and times I'll long for what once was. When that happens, I believe he understands and wraps me in his love. His protective aura surrounds me completely, just as he did in this physical world. My soul will continuously overflow with gratitude for the experience of sharing love with Tyger in its truest, most perfect form. I will always thank God for bringing us together, for knowing us better than we knew ourselves, and setting us on this path to eternity.

Life is unpredictable and only as good or as bad as we make it. We have so many opportunities to learn and with an open mind and heart, the possibilities are endless. Even in the darkest, most hopeless of circumstances, miracles can and do happen.

My prayer is this journey of ours has given you a glimpse of what lies beyond the physical connections we have to one another. As I bring my words to a close, it's important I point out although the pages of this book are ending, our story is not. It continues to be written and will go on forever. Our souls will remain connected through the thin veil that temporarily shields us from one another.

Tyger and I are bound by a love that is timeless and without limitations. There are no goodbyes for those who see with the heart. It is never goodbye, but always hello my love... always hello...

POETRY

For My Man...

A smile and a few passing words became conversations
Sharing his life experiences - Showering me with compliments
Opening my eyes to the world around ne
Helping me realize there was so much more
Nervous, cautious, unsure...
Little by little I let him in - Gaining my trust with his honesty
Making me look inside myself - Showing me what I deserved
Teaching me what it means to live
Generous, supportive, encouraging...
The Strength of a Tiger and the Heart of a Lion
Appreciation in his eyes when he looks at me
So intimate and intense when he kisses me
Passionate, focused, attentive...
So in love with this man - My lover, my friend, my protector
My heart loves him for so many reasons
Forever changed for the better by his Love

From your Pretty Baby, your "Cherry on Top"
December, 2012

I Will See You Again...

The day you left
My world turned dark and unfamiliar
Taking a breath, once so simple
Now became a constant struggle
Having to go on without our morning call
and our "I love you" texts
Without your voice, your touch, your kiss
In an instant there was silence...
Longing to see you again
Praying for strength through my despair
Clinging to the happiness you brought me
Knowing how important that was to you
Grieving for what might have been
Carrying you in my heart always
Comforted by the thought,
I will see you again...

August, 2014

Life Without You

Quietly I watch as the world continues to spin
The sun still rises and sets
Everyone going about their day
Do they realize someone is missing?
Do they notice you're no longer here?
Traffic continues to flow; people rushing to go nowhere
Time wasted on unimportant things
Slowly I walk among them, painfully aware of what's been lost
Frustrated by their hectic pace
Struggling with the simplest tasks
Totally unable to understand
How life goes on without you

September, 2014

In the Blink of an Eye

Is it possible this is my life?
Formerly full of excitement and smiles
I barely recognize it now
Who is that person in the mirror?
She once wore a glow of love and joy
Beaming and floating on air...
Now the saddest eyes are staring back
Searching for that familiar feeling
Longing for those tender moments
Holding on to precious memories
Where has he gone, the man of my dreams?
The intensity of his love fulfilled my life
My world is now so quiet and still
Forever changed the second he left us
In the blink of an eye...

October, 2014

PICTURES

~~ Mike and Diane ~~
Family reunion, July 19, 2014

"We share one heart"

~~ Our beautiful little messenger ~~

Sophia posing with an arrangement we made together for
Mikey's grave, Valentine's Day 2016

~~ Mike in the Rain ~~

Sophia's drawing, two weeks before the first anniversary of Tyger's passing. Additional drawings by Sophia can be found at: http://www.diane-santos/sophia-s-drawings

ABOUT THE AUTHOR

DIANE SANTOS, an avid reader since childhood, never once considered writing a book. Following two unsuccessful marriages, she met Mike, better known as Tyger, and together they experienced a once-in-a-lifetime love. When he passed unexpectedly, her world was shattered and she lost all desire to go on without him.

She turned to her love of reading, focusing on the subject of Near-Death Experiences (NDEs) and what actually happens when we die. Through a spiritual medium, Tyger assured her of his survival, sparking Diane's will to live again. His communications often came through song lyrics or drawings done by Sophia, her granddaughter.

Posting thoughts on social media became an outlet, and friends suggested she write a book. This was soon followed by a sign from Tyger, confirming their story had to be told. Learning about the experiences of others had given Diane hope, so sharing their ongoing journey was her opportunity to pay it forward. The title of this book describes the progression of two souls, his on one side of the veil and hers on the other. Each of them heading onward, into the light.

Born and raised in Norwich, Connecticut, Diane continues to reside there. A mother of two and grandmother of three, she works full-time as a receptionist in a physician's office. In addition to reading and writing, she also enjoys floral arranging and spending time with family. Diane can be found online:

Facebook - www.facebook.com/OnwardintoTheLight/

Website - www.diane-santos.com
(Many of Sophia's drawings are featured in the gallery section.)

Made in the USA
Charleston, SC
15 April 2016